LOVE AT FIRST BITE

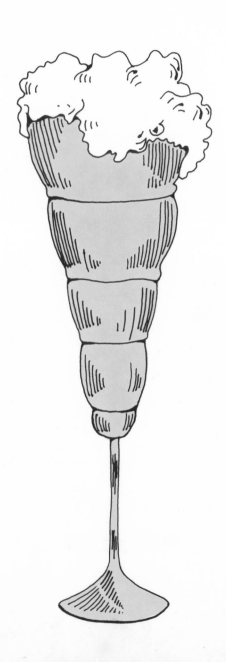

LOVE AT FIRST BITE

SNACKS AND MEALTIME TREATS
THE QUICK AND EASY WAY

By

JANE COOPER

Designed and Illustrated by

SHERRY STREETER

Alfred A. Knopf  New York

A
SPECIAL THANKS
TO
PAT ROSS
AND
WENDY WOLF

and Grace Clark

Text Copyright © 1977 by Jane Cooper
Illustrations Copyright © 1977 by Sherry Streeter
All rights reserved under International and Pan-American Copyright
Conventions. Published in the United States by Alfred A. Knopf, Inc.,
New York, and simultaneously in Canada by Random House of Canada
Limited, Toronto. Distributed by Random House, Inc., New York.

Library of Congress Cataloging in Publication Data
Cooper, Jane, 1946-
Love at first bite.
SUMMARY: Presents easy recipes that use basic
cooking techniques and need little adult supervision.
1. Cookery—Juvenile literature. [1. Cookery]
I. Streeter, Sherry II. Title.
TX652.5.C65 1977   641.5   76-42246
ISBN 0-394-83399-6   ISBN 0-394-93399-0 lib. bdg.

Manufactured in the United States of America

FOR
FLIP & TJ
WITH
LOVE

CONTENTS

LAUNCHING A TASTY ADVENTURE

How much time have you spent waiting for someone *else* to make breakfast? Or eating an ordinary, dull school lunch? Or craving a great new dessert—and getting lumpy chocolate pudding instead? After all this, isn't it time you learned how to make all these things for yourself?

Cooking is something everyone can do and enjoy. Once you've learned a few basic techniques, such as measuring and chopping, cooking your own food can become a delicious way to expand your imagination and independence. You'll soon find that cooking is more than just following a recipe—it's an adventure. If there's an ingredient you don't like in a recipe, you can often take it out and substitute something you do like. Experiment and improvise—it's all part of the secret of good cooking. You'll soon be transforming ordinary peanut-butter sandwiches into extraordinary extravaganzas!

This book is a guide to help you prepare tasty, healthy, and quick foods for when you're really hungry and want something right away. You won't find menus for five-course meals, but you will find ideas for breakfasts, bag lunches, afternoon snacks, drinks, and desserts—all no-bake. There are enough ideas and suggestions to satisfy your appetite for a long time, and to launch you on your own tasty adventures. So give it a try—delicious rewards guaranteed!

Before you start, always get permission to use the kitchen if no adults are at home. These recipes are all safe to make if the ordinary kitchen precautions are observed, but you should not attempt to cook alone until you get the okay from your parents.

GETTING STARTED

1. Read the whole recipe first. Make sure you have every ingredient and the equipment you need, and that you understand all the instructions.
2. Assemble all the ingredients and equipment near your working space.
3. Wear an apron if you've got on good clothes. Keep a dish towel or paper towels nearby to wipe your hands on, and a sponge or paper towels for spills.
4. Wash your hands.

WHILE YOU'RE COOKING

1. Measure the ingredients carefully and follow all instructions in order.
2. Wash and dry all fruits and vegetables thoroughly in cold water.
3. Keep pot holders handy. You'll need them to hold onto saucepans while stirring and to remove hot pans from the stove.
4. Turn saucepan and skillet handles away from the edge of the stove so that there will be no accidental bumps or spills.
5. Never place an empty pot or pan over heat—unless it's cast-iron.
6. Plug in all electrical appliances with *dry* hands.
7. Wipe up any spills as soon as they happen.

AFTER IT'S OVER

1. Make sure the stove is turned off!
2. Wash all your dishes. It's much easier to clean things before the food dries and hardens.
3. Unplug all electric appliances, and wipe them carefully with a damp cloth.
4. Return ingredients back to the shelves where you found them.
5. Store leftover perishables (foods that are likely to spoil or decay) in the refrigerator. Cover them with wax paper or place them in a plastic box with a tight-fitting lid. A secure cover will prevent your food from absorbing odors from the refrigerator—and prevent the refrigerator from absorbing odors from your food.

IN CASE OF EMERGENCY

1. If you get burned, keep the burn under cold running water. Do not put butter or grease on it—the cold water helps take the heat out, the butter keeps it in. Find out where the first-aid or burn ointment is kept, and use it.
2. If there is a grease fire on the stove, quickly smother it with baking soda, salt, or if it's very small, put a saucepan lid over it. Never douse it with water, which causes a grease fire to spread.

   Many families now keep small fire extinguishers in their kitchen as an extra safety precaution. If you don't have one, you might talk to your parents about investing in one—they are inexpensive, and can be very important to have around.
3. If you cut yourself, keep the cut under cold running water, then place a clean bandage over it, to keep other things (like salt) from getting into the cut. If it's a serious gash, show an adult and/or call a doctor.

EQUIPMENT YOU WILL NEED

You'll probably find most of this equipment in your kitchen already. If you don't have something, like an apple corer or an electric frying pan, you don't have to go out and buy it—improvise with another piece you do have.

APPLE CORER

Apples can be cored with a knife, but this makes the job easier. Set the apple on a wooden cutting board. Stick the apple corer into the center of the apple, and turn and push it all the way through. The core should come out when the apple corer is removed, but if it doesn't, push it out with your finger.

CHEESECLOTH

This is a thin, loosely woven cotton cloth which is sold by the package in most hardware and kitchen supply stores.

COOKIE SHEET

These are rectangular or square sheets of metal to use for baking and—in this cookbook—as a surface for making some of the Sweet Snacks.

CUTTING BOARD

Cutting boards are made out of wood and are designed in many different shapes and sizes. Use them as a cutting surface for food, rather than scarring the kitchen counter or table.

DOUBLE BOILER

Use this to heat foods such as chocolate and milk that scorch or burn easily when they are cooked directly over a stove burner. Fill the bottom half of the double boiler one-third full with water, and bring it to a boil. Set the top half, into which you put the food, over the boiling water. This makes enough heat to cook the food without burning it. Just make sure all the water doesn't boil away or the bottom pan will burn.

EGG BEATER

Use this to beat egg whites stiff and to whip cream. Before using it, place a damp cloth under the bowl to keep it from jiggling around.

ELECTRIC BLENDER

An electric blender can be used to chop, grind, blend, and whip. Always put the lid on it before turning it on, and *never* stick spoons, spatulas, or fingers into the blender jar when the blender is whizzing.

This is very helpful for cooking pancakes and pan cookies, where steady, even heat is important. Turn the temperature dial to desired setting.

ELECTRIC FRYING PAN

ELECTRIC MIXER

If you have a lot to mix in a little time, or are just low on energy, this is quicker and easier then cranking an eggbeater's blades. It's especially good for stirring pancake batter, beating egg whites, and whipping cream. Remember not to lift the moving blades of the electric mixer above the rim of the bowl, or you'll decorate yourself and the room with whatever you're mixing.

Use the side with large holes for grating cheese, apples, and carrots. Use the side with small holes for grating orange peel, lemon peel, and nutmeg. Place waxed paper underneath it to catch the grated food. Press the food against the grater and rub it across the holes in short, firm strokes—but don't grate your fingers!

GRATER

KNIVES

A French chef's knife is long and thick-bladed. It's excellent for slicing vegetables and chopping nuts, but keep it away from your fingers. A bread knife has a sawtooth edge which cuts bread without tearing it. A paring knife is small but sharp and is useful for cutting fresh fruits, vegetables, and dried fruits.

There are two types of measuring cups: liquid and dry. Dry measuring cups are used for solid ingredients such as flour, butter, and cream cheese. Fill the right size cup to the top, then level off the measured ingredient with the straight edge of a knife. Liquid measuring cups are used for ingredients such as milk, vegetable oil, and honey. Pour the liquid into the cup to the desired level. When pouring out liquid, if any sticks to the sides of the cup, scrape it out with a rubber spatula.

MEASURING CUPS

MEASURING SPOONS

For dry ingredients like baking powder, dry mustard, and flour, dip the size spoon you need into the container and level off the measured ingredient with the straight edge of a knife. Ingredients such as vegetable oil and salt should be slowly poured to the top of the spoon.

These come in different sizes, holding anything from two cups to sixteen cups. Just be sure to use a bowl large enough to comfortably contain all your ingredients, with room to mix without spilling.

MIXING BOWLS

MIXING SPOONS

These can be made out of metal, plastic, or wood. Good cooks recommend wooden spoons for creaming, beating, and stirring. Metal spoons are useful for stirring food that is cooking.

PIE PLATE

This is a round, shallow pan that can be made of ovenproof glass, aluminum, or tin. The most common size is nine inches in diameter (across the top).

SAUCEPANS

These come in different sizes. Some are small enough for melting butter, others are large enough for making soup. Choose the size saucepan which will contain your food with room to stir without spilling over.

SKILLETS OR FRYING PANS

These come in many sizes, to hold one fried egg or eight pancakes. Choose the right size for your ingredients.

SLOTTED SPOON

Use this to remove and drain solid foods cooked or suspended in a liquid.

SPATULAS

There are two types of spatulas, metal and rubber. A metal spatula is used to flip pancakes and lift fried eggs. A rubber spatula is used to scrape food out of mixing bowls, electric blender jars, and saucepans. Never leave a rubber spatula sitting in a pan while foods are cooking or you may add some melted rubber to the pot.

STRAINER

Wire strainers are used to drain foods that are cooked in liquid, such as hard-boiled eggs, or packed in it, such as canned fruits. If you plan to save the liquid, set the strainer over a bowl before you pour the food and liquid into it. Otherwise, place it over the sink.

VEGETABLE PEELER

This is easier to use than a knife to remove the skins from fruits and vegetables such as apples, pears, carrots, and potatoes. (It also sharpens pencils.) Press the peeler against whatever you want to skin and scrape *away* from your other hand.

WIRE WHISK

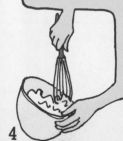

Use this to beat liquid ingredients such as eggs, yogurt, honey, and oil. Small whisks are used for beating sauces and batters. Big balloon whisks are used for whipping egg whites.

BEAT

Stir a mixture smooth with a regular, hard movement.

BEAT EGG WHITES

Separate yolks from whites and have eggs at room temperature. Turn the eggbeater blades steadily and quickly—or use an electric mixer—until the egg whites are shiny and stiff. (If using a hand beater, your arm will probably also get stiff, as this takes about three or four minutes.) The egg whites should form small peaks when the beater is lifted out of the bowl.

BLEND

Mix thoroughly two or more ingredients.

BOIL

Heat liquid (for these recipes, water is the only thing you'll need to boil) in a saucepan to the point that bubbles form on the bottom and break on the surface. When all the liquid is in motion, it is boiling.

CHOP DRIED FRUIT

Use scissors. To keep the fruit from sticking to the blades, dip the blades every so often in warm water. You can also use a paring knife. Put the fruit on a cutting board and cut it into small pieces.

CHOP NUTS

Some softer kinds of nuts, like pecans, cashews, and walnuts, can be broken by hand or cut with scissors. Others, like almonds, filberts, and Brazil nuts, must be chopped with a large knife. Spread the nuts on a cutting board. Hold the point of knife on the cutting board with one hand and move the blade up and down through the nuts with the other. Another way is to put the nuts in a sturdy bag (paper or plastic will work), close the opening with a rubber band, and smash the nuts with a hammer or wooden mallet.

COAT

Roll or stir food in nuts, shredded coconut, seeds, wheat germ, or whatever, until all the sides are evenly covered.

CREAM

Work together solid fats, like butter, margarine, or shortening, with sugar, forming a soft, even mixture. The solid fat should first be warmed to room temperature so that it's more easily blended with the sugar.

CRUSH GARLIC

Take a clove of garlic, which is one of the many sections of a head of garlic, and press down on it with the flat side of a knife. The skin will peel off easily. If you want small pieces of garlic, chop the clove with the knife or put it through a garlic press. Crush as many cloves as the recipe calls for, one clove at a time.

FOLD

This term is used when mixing light and fluffy ingredients, such as stiffly beaten egg whites, into heavier ones, like pastry or egg batters. Make sure the batter is in a large mixing bowl. Pour on top the light ingredients and work them into the batter by cutting through the center of the entire mixture with a rubber spatula, bringing it up the sides of the bowl, and folding the batter over toward the center. Continue cutting and folding until the two elements are thoroughly blended.

GREASE A PAN OR SKILLET

With a scrap of wax paper, rub a small amount of butter or vegetable oil on pan or skillet until the entire surface is lightly covered.

MELT BUTTER

Put the measured amount of butter in a small saucepan and place over *low* heat. As soon as the butter becomes liquid, remove the pan from the burner. Butter burns very easily.

SCALD

Heat a liquid to just below the boiling point. To scald milk, heat the measured amount in a saucepan over medium heat until a skinlike layer forms on the top and tiny bubbles ring the edge of the pan.

SEPARATE AN EGG

You'll need a round-tipped knife and two small bowls.

1. Take the egg out of the refrigerator (cold eggs separate better). Over one of the bowls, crack the egg in the center of the shell with the flat edge of the knife. Don't hit too hard or you'll have a mess in your hands.
2. Press your thumbs in the middle of the crack and carefully pull the shell apart. Tilt the egg upright so that the yolk stays in one half and most of the white in the other.
3. Pour the white into the bowl. Now move the yolk back and forth between the shells so that the remaining white falls into the bowl.
4. Pour the yolk into the other bowl.
5. If you plan to beat the egg whites, do not let any of the yolk get mixed in. The tiniest amount will prevent the white from beating well. If some of the yolk does get mixed in with the white, the empty eggshell works best for removing it.

SIMMER

Boil liquid very slowly over low heat.

STIR

Mix in a circular motion until all ingredients are worked together.

TOAST SESAME SEEDS

Put measured amount of seeds in a small frying pan, cover with a lid, and place over medium heat. Gently shake the pan back and forth over the burner until the seeds start to pop. (They almost sound like popcorn.) Continue cooking and shaking for about 30 seconds, or until the popping stops, and remove the pan from heat.

WHIP CREAM

Use chilled, heavy cream. (For best results, first chill the mixing bowl for about one hour.) Pour cream into mixing bowl and beat with an electric mixer that is set on the indicated speed. Beat until the cream stands in soft peaks whose tips just fall over. Another way, but a lot more work, is to use an eggbeater. Turn the eggbeater blades steadily until the cream stands in peaks. One cup heavy cream makes two cups whipped cream.

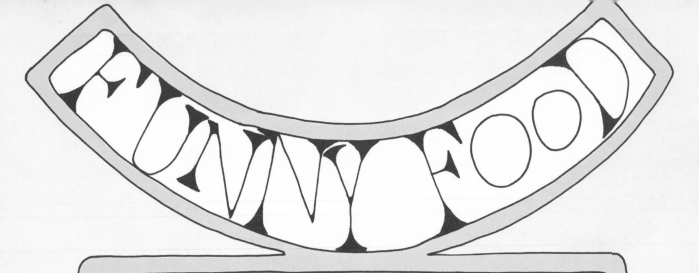

FUNNY FOOD

You'll already have most of the ingredients listed in these recipes, or you can easily find them in the supermarket. But some might be unfamiliar. If you can't find them in your cupboard or on your grocer's shelf, they can be found in most health-food stores.

APPLE & PEACH BUTTER

These are similar to fruit sauces, like applesauce, only they are thicker and darker . . . and they don't contain butter! They are used as spreads on toast, pancakes, and sandwiches, but try them on other foods, like yogurt and oatmeal.

CAROB POWDER

It looks like cocoa, tastes like cocoa, but—you guessed it—it's not cocoa. It's the ground fruit of the carob tree, an evergreen that grows around the Mediterranean Sea. This nutritious fruit has been eaten since Biblical times and is a healthy substitute for cocoa.

FLAVOR EXTRACTS

Flavorings such as vanilla, almond, orange, lemon, and mint should have the word "pure" written on the label. This means that the flavor comes from that particular fruit or nut. The "artificially" flavored extracts use chemicals to give them their flavor. It's best to avoid these.

LEMON JUICE

Squeeze it from real lemons, not from bottles of concentrated juice. Real lemon juice is not only tastier, but healthier as well. To tell a good lemon, test the skin. If it is thin and smooth, there will be a lot of juice. If the skin is thick and rough, the lemon will be harder to squeeze and will give less juice. Lemons kept at room temperature will give more juice than ones stored in the refrigerator.

SEEDS

These are storehouses of vitamins and minerals because each one is equipped with the energy needed for the growth of a new plant—only we get to them first! Seeds such as poppy, dill, sesame, and caraway are delicious seasonings for other foods. Pine, pumpkin, and sunflower seeds taste good enough to be eaten by themselves, raw or toasted, and are also great additions to foods such as cookies, yogurt, salads, and breads.

SORGHUM

This thick, dark, sweet syrup is made from cereal grains. It is a delicious substitute for molasses, maple syrup, or honey.

TAHINI

A paste made from ground sesame seeds, this is a great favorite in the Middle East. Because of its strong flavor, it is usually mixed with other foods, like honey and chick-peas.

TIGER'S MILK

No, it's not milk from a tiger. It is a powderlike nutrition booster which is usually added to milk. It comes in a variety of flavors.

WHEAT GERM

The heart or germinating part of the wheat berry is the major source of vitamins, minerals, and protein in whole-wheat flour. Wheat germ can be eaten raw or toasted. Because it contains oil, wheat germ should be stored in the refrigerator to prevent it from becoming rancid.

YOGURT

Yogurt is a tangy, custardlike "cultured milk." This means it is a milk that has been soured by a special bacteria. Yogurt is nutritionally superior to plain milk; it aids digestion and helps keep the intestines healthy. Yogurt is not only eaten all by itself, but it mixes well in pancake batters, with granola, and with fruit as a dessert. It's also a healthy substitute for sour cream.

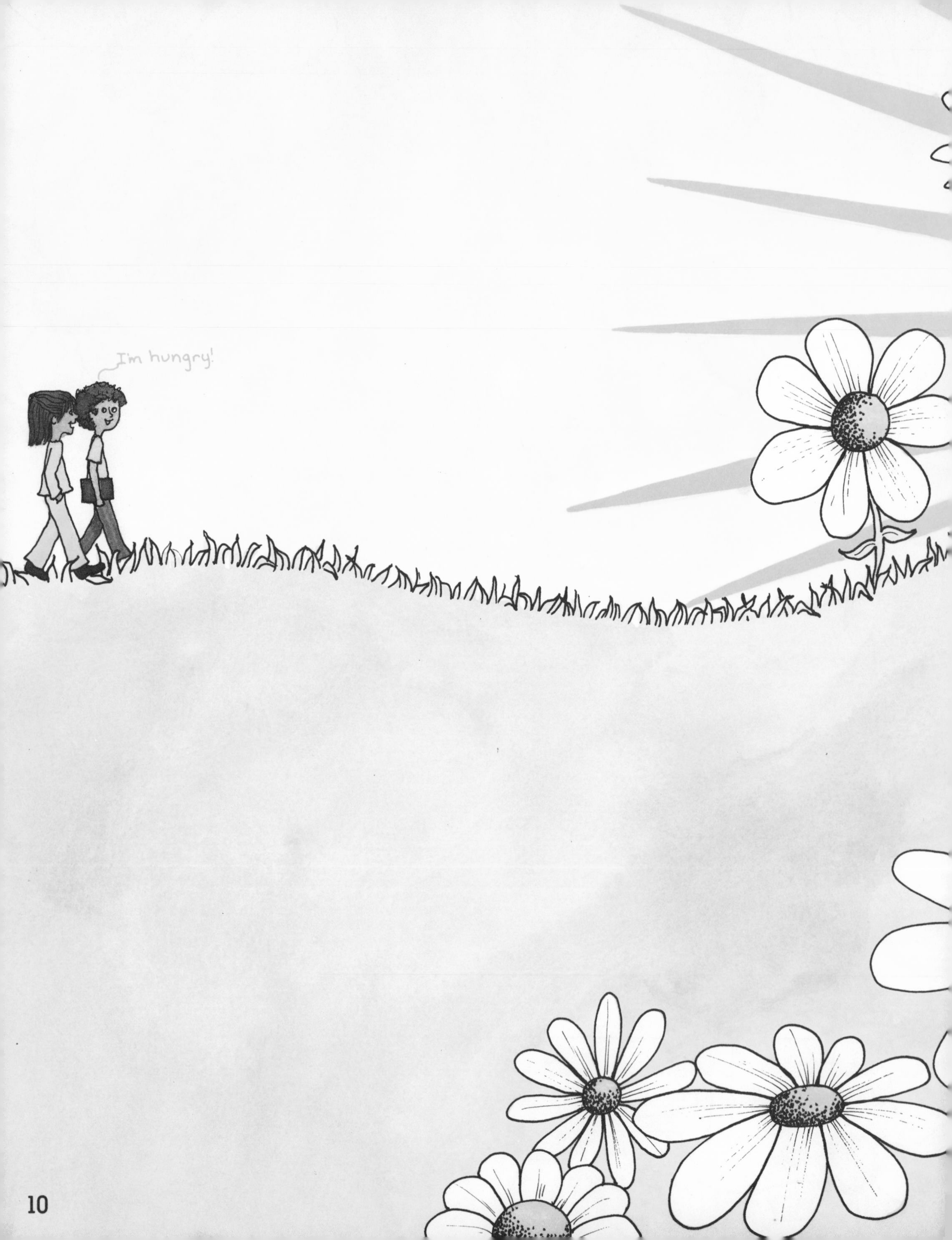
I'm hungry!

MORNING GLORIES

MAKING YOUR OWN BREAKFASTS

YAWN

You can have a different flavor every morning—and still get lots of energy—with these quick, tasty, and nourishing breakfasts. Whether you're going to school, on a hike, or into the next room to watch TV, it's more important to eat a good breakfast than any other meal. And, as you'll discover, breakfast can be much more fun than just opening up a box of cereal and a carton of milk.

NO-BLUNDER BLENDER BREAKFASTS

Everything that you'll need for instant energy and a full stomach can be put into the blender jar, whizzed around, and then poured into a glass. Each recipe makes enough for one big, healthy breakfast.

Equipment for all blender recipes:
electric blender
measuring cup
measuring spoons

Method for all blender recipes:
1. Measure all ingredients and put them into the blender jar.
2. Blend at medium speed about 10 seconds or until everything is well mixed.

SUNRISE SPECIAL
1 cup fruit nectar
4 or 5 pineapple chunks
$\frac{1}{2}$ cup dry milk powder
or yogurt
sprinkle of ginger

FLIPPED OUT FRUIT
1 cup yogurt
1 cup chopped fruit—
peaches, papaya, berries,
or other
4 tsps. honey

MILKSHOE SHAKE
Whiz this one a little longer—about 30 seconds.
$1\frac{1}{4}$ cups milk
1 banana, broken into
small chunks
$\frac{1}{4}$ cup unsalted cashews
1 Tbsp. sweetener—
honey, molasses,
or maple syrup
1 egg yolk or $\frac{1}{4}$ cup dry
milk powder

SUPER TIGER NOG
1 cup milk
$\frac{1}{2}$ cup Tiger's Milk
$\frac{1}{4}$ tsp. flavor extract—
vanilla, peppermint,
orange, or other

APE SHAKE
1 cup milk
$\frac{1}{2}$ cup yogurt
1 Tbsp. honey or
molasses
1 banana, broken into
small chunks

BERRY GOOD

1¼ cups milk
¼ cup dry milk powder
½ cup berries—
strawberries,
raspberries,
blueberries, or other
1 Tbsp. honey

MORNING MMMM

1 cup yogurt
1 banana, broken into
small chunks
½ cup canned crushed
pineapple

TIGERS & FRUIT

1 cup milk
½ cup Tiger's Milk
1 cup sliced fruit—
apple, pear, mango,
banana, or other

WAKE-UP SHAKE-UP

½ cup milk
¼ cup dry milk powder
1 cup fruit juice—
grape, apple, pineapple,
or other

CHOCOLATEEARLY

1¼ cups milk
1 Tbsp. cocoa or carob
2 tsps. honey or
maple syrup
¼ tsp. cinnamon
dash of salt

TROPICAL TIGER

1 cup juice—cranberry,
orange, grape, or other
½ cup Tiger's Milk
1 tsp. honey or
maple syrup
sprinkle of ginger

13

Because eggs are nature's most perfect protein food—and protein is so important for starting the day—fix them any way you like and enjoy them every week. You'll be making an almost perfect breakfast.

EGG BREAKFASTS

Each recipe makes one serving.

Always use fresh eggs.

Cook eggs over low heat.

Never use an egg that has cracked or that has a strong, stale smell.

SCRAMBLED EGGS

Equipment:

small frying pan
small mixing bowl
measuring spoons
wooden mixing spoon

Ingredients:

2 eggs
1 tsp. water
1 Tbsp. butter

Method:

1. Break eggs into mixing bowl and add water. Beat lightly.
2. If you want, add any Tasty Additions and mix them in well.
3. Melt butter in frying pan over low heat.
4. Pour eggs into the pan and stir just enough to keep them from sticking to the bottom of the pan.
5. When eggs have thickened, but still look moist, they've finished cooking. Serve them alone or on buttered toast, roll, or English muffin.

EGG SHAKE

Add one raw egg yolk to any favorite blender drink or milkshake. Don't worry about the yolk tasting yukky . . . it gives the drink a richer, more delicious flavor and will give you a lot more protein and vitamins. Try it!

ANOTHER EGG SHAKE

EGGS MAKE AN EGGSEPTIONALLY EGGSELLENT BREAKFAST & ARE EGGSACTLY WHAT YOU NEED FOR EGGSTRA ENERGY IF YOU ARE EGGSPECTING AN EGGSTREMELY EGGSITING OR EGGSHAUSTING DAY.

Here are some scrambled ideas for more scrumptious scrambled eggs. Unscramble the underlined words then add one or more to your scrambles.

☆ CHOPPED VEGETABLES - <u>ONINO</u>, <u>MOTATO</u>, <u>LECERY</u>, <u>MUSHMOORS</u>
☆ SOUR <u>CRMEA</u> AND <u>CHEVIS</u> OR <u>TARRANOG</u> OR <u>RAPSLEY</u>
☆ TOASTED <u>SASEME</u> OR <u>FUNSLOWER</u> SEEDS
☆ COTTAGE <u>SHEECE</u>   ☆ <u>GREATD</u> <u>SHEEEC</u>
☆ CRUMBLED <u>CABON</u>   ☆ <u>OYS</u> SAUCE   ☆ <u>NEAB</u> SPROUTS

POACHED EGG

Equipment:
- small frying pan
- small bowl
- timer or clock
- measuring spoons
- slotted spoon

Ingredients:
- 1 egg
- ½ tsp. salt
- 1 tsp. vinegar

Method:
1. Put enough water in the frying pan to cover an egg, about 2 inches deep.
2. Add salt and vinegar to water and bring to a boil.
3. Break the egg very gently into a small bowl. Turn the stove burner to the lowest setting and gently slip the egg into the hot water.
4. Set the timer for 3 to 5 minutes. The egg will be cooked when the white part is firm.
5. Remove egg with the slotted spoon, being careful not to break the yolk, and serve in a dish or on a piece of buttered toast.
6. Now if you want, sprinkle one of the Tasty Additions on the egg.

BOILED EGG

Equipment:
- small saucepan with cover
- timer or clock
- strainer

Ingredients:
- 1 egg
- ¼ tsp. salt

Method:
1. Place egg in saucepan and cover with cold water. Add salt to water. Cover pan.
2. Place pan over medium-high heat and bring water to a boil.
3. Immediately reduce the heat so that water simmers, and set timer for:
   - very soft-boiled.... 2 mins.
   - soft-boiled........ 3 mins.
   - medium-boiled .... 5 mins.
   - hard-boiled .... 10 mins.
4. When the egg has cooked, remove saucepan from stove and pour egg into the strainer. Rinse the egg under cold running water for about 10 seconds.
5. Crack shell open and spoon out the egg, if soft. If hard-boiled, simply peel. Serve soft to medium eggs with:

For tastier boiled or poached eggs, sprinkle with one of these:

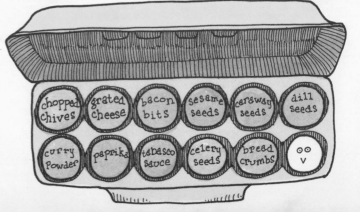

chopped chives, grated cheese, bacon bits, sesame seeds, caraway seeds, dill seeds, curry powder, paprika, tabasco sauce, celery seeds, bread crumbs

FRIED EGG

Equipment:
- small frying pan
- small bowl or saucer
- metal spatula
- measuring spoons

Ingredients:
- 1 egg
- 1 Tbsp. butter

Tasty Additions:
- 1 Tbsp. grated cheese
- 1 Tbsp. bread crumbs
- 1 tsp. herbs—parsley, tarragon, basil, or chives
- 1 Tbsp. heavy cream
- 2 Tbsps. crumbled bacon or sausage
- 2 Tbsps. chopped tomato

Method:
1. Melt butter in frying pan over low heat.
2. Break egg into bowl, then carefully slip into frying pan.
3. Add any Tasty Additions you'd like. Sprinkle or pour them over egg.
4. Cook egg until the white part is firm. Remove the egg with spatula.
5. Serve with buttered toast, roll, or English muffin.

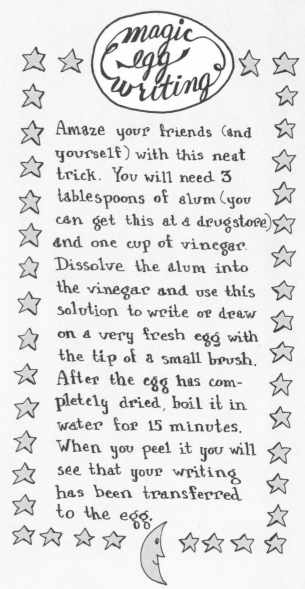

magic egg writing

Amaze your friends (and yourself) with this neat trick. You will need 3 tablespoons of alum (you can get this at a drugstore) and one cup of vinegar. Dissolve the alum into the vinegar and use this solution to write or draw on a very fresh egg with the tip of a small brush. After the egg has completely dried, boil it in water for 15 minutes. When you peel it you will see that your writing has been transferred to the egg.

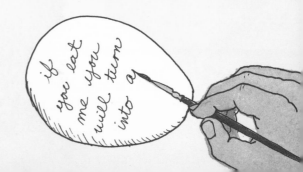

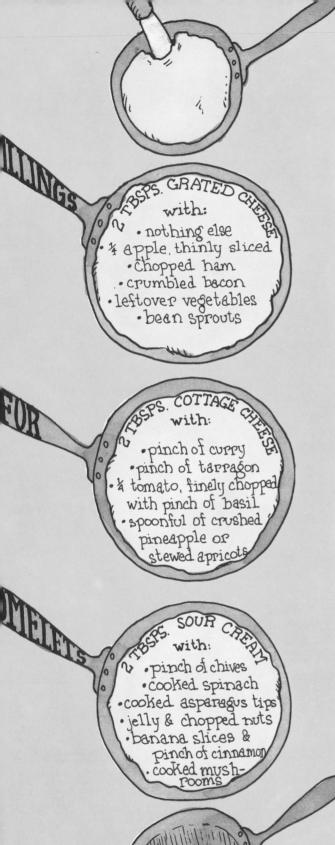

FILLINGS FOR OMELETS

2 TBSPS. GRATED CHEESE with:
- nothing else
- ¼ apple, thinly sliced
- chopped ham
- crumbled bacon
- leftover vegetables
- bean sprouts

2 TBSPS. COTTAGE CHEESE with:
- pinch of curry
- pinch of tarragon
- ¼ tomato, finely chopped with pinch of basil
- spoonful of crushed pineapple or stewed apricots

2 TBSPS. SOUR CREAM with:
- pinch of chives
- cooked spinach
- cooked asparagus tips
- jelly & chopped nuts
- banana slices & pinch of cinnamon
- cooked mushrooms

OMELET

Equipment:

1 small skillet, about 7 inches across, with lid
small mixing bowl
measuring spoons
fork or wire whisk
metal spatula

Ingredients:

2 eggs
1 Tbsp. cold water
1 Tbsp. butter

Method:

1. Break the eggs into the mixing bowl, add the water, and beat until the whites and yolks are well blended.
2. Place the skillet over medium-high heat and wait for the skillet to get very hot. Add the butter and swirl it around so that it coats the bottom and sides of the pan. As soon as the foam subsides but before the butter browns, add the eggs.
3. Rotate the skillet so that the eggs spread evenly to the sides.
4. As the omelet cooks, use the spatula to lift the edges of the cooked egg. Tilt skillet so that the uncooked portion on top runs underneath. Continue lifting and tilting until the top side is no longer runny and the bottom side is light brown.
5. Spread one of the Omelet Fillings over the eggs, turn heat to low, cover, and let the eggs cook a minute longer.
6. Remove the lid. Loosen one half of the omelet and fold it over the other half. Remove the skillet from the stove and slide the omelet onto a plate. Serve it with any kind of breakfast bread.

An omelet also makes a great lunch or dinner.

TOAD-IN-A-HOLE

This breakfast can be as interesting as the kinds of bread you use. Look at the Incredible Sandwich List (page 33) for different ideas. Also try adding a little grated cheese to the egg while it's cooking. It's great! And don't worry—these eggs won't give you warts.

Equipment:
    small skillet
    water glass
    small dish
    measuring spoons
    metal spatula

Ingredients:
    1 slice of bread, any kind
    1 egg
    2 Tbsps. butter

Method:
1. Use the rim of the glass to cut a hole in the center of the bread. Remove the round cut.
2. Break the egg into the small dish.
3. Put the skillet over low-medium heat and melt the butter.
4. Add the bread and let it cook until the bottom is crispy and golden-brown.
5. Turn the bread over, and slip the egg into the hole.
6. When the egg is firm, lift the bread and egg together and transfer to a plate.

Rinse egg-caked dishes in cold water. Hot water hardens the protein and makes it more difficult to remove.

To test an egg for freshness, place it in a deep cup of water. If the egg sinks and lies on its side, it's fresh. If the large end rises slightly, it is a little stale. If the egg stands on end or floats, throw it out.

The Masai, a group of people from Kenya and Tanzania, regard eggs as being unfit to eat. However, they think nothing of drinking blood.

To tell if an egg is raw or hard-boiled, spin it on a flat surface. If it spins very fast and easily, it is hard-boiled. Raw eggs wobble and barely spin at all.

Remember to never cook an egg in or over high heat. It will make it rubbery.

Use half of the empty eggshell to remove any shell fragments floating in an egg you've cracked open. This works better than a spoon.

There is no difference between a brown and a white egg...except the color, of course.

CEREAL BREAKFASTS

Homemade Granola

Granola looks, pours, and crunches like a cereal—and in fact, *is* a cereal. But it's a cereal with a difference . . . it tastes good *and* it's good for you! Here is a way to make your own granola. You can change the recipe around any way you like. This recipe makes enough for *lots* of breakfasts.

How would you like a change from those puffed, fluffed, rainbow-colored cereals? Here are some good, down-to-earth breakfast cereals. They'll keep your energy up and your hunger down.

large
mixing bowl

measuring
cup

measuring
spoons

large, heavy
skillet

2 cups
uncooked
oatmeal

½ cup
shredded
coconut

½ cup
wheat germ

½ cup
chopped,
unsalted nuts

½ cup
chopped
dried fruit

½ cup honey,
molasses,
or maple syrup

½ cup
vegetable
oil

¼ cup
sunflower
seeds

¼ cup additional seeds

1 tsp.
cinnamon

¼ tsp.
nutmeg

Method:

1. Measure and mix all ingredients, *except* dried fruit, in mixing bowl.
2. Stir mixture until the oil and honey coat the rest of the ingredients.
3. Pour this mixture into the large skillet and place over medium heat.
4. Stir mixture constantly for about 5 minutes, or until oatmeal turns a golden-brown color.
5. Remove skillet from heat and stir in dried fruit.
6. Allow granola to cool, and store for future breakfasts and snacks in a can or jar with a tight-fitting lid.

SPECIAL
UNCOOKED
GRANOLA
MIX

Mix together
all ingredients,
except oil
and honey.
Store in
a clean jar.

for
CRUNCHIER
granola,
add
more
nuts

for
SWEETER
granola,
add more
honey, molasses
or maple syrup

for
CHEWIER
granola,
add more
dried fruits

21

BANANA QUICK

¾ cup toasted wheat germ
or uncooked oatmeal
¼ cup chopped dried fruit
—raisins, apricots,
apples, pitted prunes,
or other
1 banana, sliced

APPLE QUICK

1 cup toasted wheat germ
or uncooked oatmeal
1 apple, sliced
½ cup applesauce
¼ cup chopped nuts—
walnuts, pecans, peanuts,
or other
sprinkle of cinnamon

YOGURT QUICK

½ cup toasted wheat germ
or uncooked oatmeal
1 cup yogurt
½ cup sliced fresh fruit
—peach, berries, banana,
or other

SERVES 2

Equipment for all Quick recipes:
measuring cup
serving bowl

Method for all Quick recipes:
1. Measure ingredients into serving bowl
   and mix together.
2. Top with milk and sweeten with honey,
   maple syrup, brown sugar, or molasses.

QUICK CEREAL MIXES

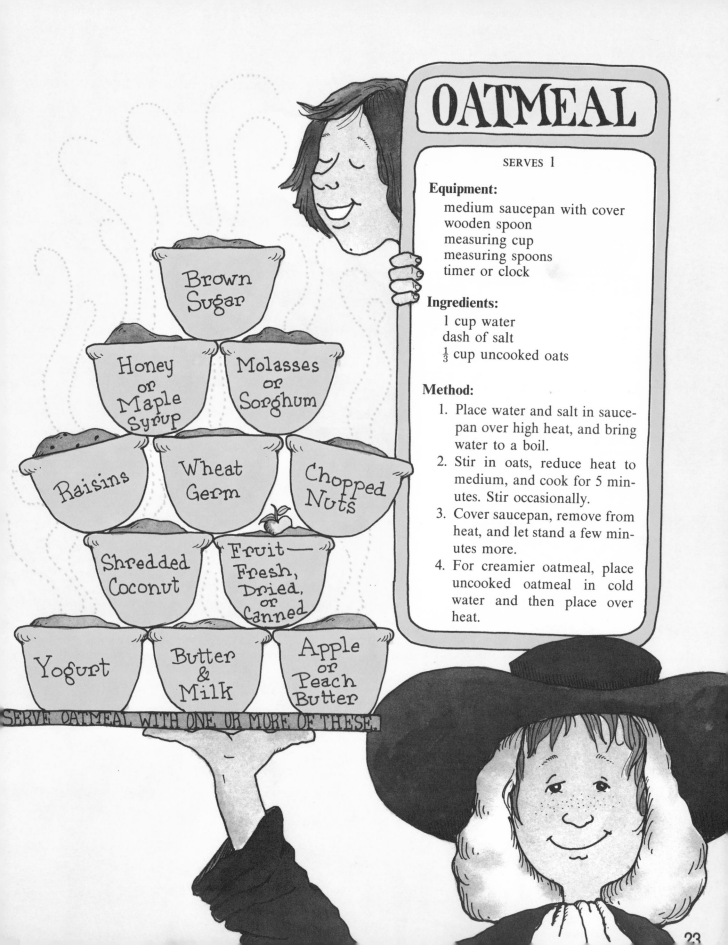

OATMEAL

SERVES 1

Equipment:
medium saucepan with cover
wooden spoon
measuring cup
measuring spoons
timer or clock

Ingredients:
1 cup water
dash of salt
$\frac{1}{3}$ cup uncooked oats

Method:
1. Place water and salt in saucepan over high heat, and bring water to a boil.
2. Stir in oats, reduce heat to medium, and cook for 5 minutes. Stir occasionally.
3. Cover saucepan, remove from heat, and let stand a few minutes more.
4. For creamier oatmeal, place uncooked oatmeal in cold water and then place over heat.

Brown Sugar

Honey or Maple Syrup

Molasses or Sorghum

Raisins

Wheat Germ

Chopped Nuts

Shredded Coconut

Fruit— Fresh, Dried, or Canned

Yogurt

Butter & Milk

Apple or Peach Butter

SERVE OATMEAL WITH ONE OR MORE OF THESE.

It's perfectly okay to start the day with dessert—if it's yogurt. It's a pudding, it's a sundae, it's delicious! You can make your own at home for an ever-ready supply, and add anything from maple syrup to peanuts to make it taste just the way you like. There is only one important point to remember when making yogurt at home: it takes yogurt to make yogurt. To start your own batch, you must already have some on hand.

Equipment:
    large saucepan
    measuring cup
    measuring spoons
    mixing spoon
    quart jar with lid
    medium-sized towel

Ingredients:
    1 quart whole or nonfat milk
    ¼ cup dry milk powder
    1 Tbsp. yogurt

Method:

1. Preheat oven to 200°.
2. Place milk in saucepan over low heat until scalding. Watch carefully to be sure the milk does not boil over.
3. Remove saucepan from heat and add powdered milk. Stir in very well.
4. Let the milk cool to lukewarm (when it's warm but not hot to the touch) and then add the yogurt. Stir very, very well. (For an incredibly creamy yogurt, use an electric blender to mix the ingredients.) Pour milk into quart jar.
5. Wrap quart jar in the towel, stick it in the oven, then turn oven off *immediately*. Too much heat will kill the yogurt bacteria.
6. From 4 to 8 hours later, you have yogurt. The longer the yogurt is left in the oven, the tarter it is; 4-hour yogurt is sweeter. Refrigerate as soon as you remove it from oven.
7. Be sure to save 1 tablespoon from this batch to start your next.

For a sweet, custard-like yogurt, add 1 tsp. vanilla extract or 2 Tbsps. honey or maple syrup to the hot milk. Stir in at the same time as you add the dried milk powder.

FOR BREAKFAST

MAPLE S**Y**RUP
H**O**NEY
WHEAT **G**ERM
APPLESA**U**CE
G**R**ANOLA
WALNU**T**S

RA**I**SINS
SESAME **S**EEDS

b**R**OWN SUGAR
MOLASS**E**S
PE**A**CHES
PINEAPP**L**E
b**L**UEBERRIES
CHOCOLATE S**Y**RUP

FIGS
STR**A**WBERRIES
PECA**N**S
NU**T**MEG
VANILL**A** EXTRACT
ALMOND**S**
APPLE BU**T**TER
C**I**NNAMON

Just about everything tastes good with yogurt.
Try one or more of these ingredients in your next bowl of yogurt for breakfast.

26

PANCAKE BREAKFASTS

TIP-TOP PANCAKE TOPPINGS:

Pancakes may stack up the flavor, but they take a little more time to make—so save them for a morning when you're not in a hurry, like on a weekend. They're delicious for special occasions like birthdays, too.

maple syrup, honey, molasses, or sorghum

apple butter or peach butter

sliced fresh fruit and powdered sugar

lemon juice and powdered sugar or honey

sour cream and berries

applesauce and cinnamon

nut butters
—peanut butter, almond butter, cashew butter, or other

strawberries, or other fruit, and whipped cream

crushed berries mixed with honey

Combine over low heat

$\frac{1}{2}$ cup butter,
$\frac{1}{2}$ cup brown sugar.
When melted, add
$\frac{1}{2}$ cup chopped nuts

Combine over low heat

$\frac{1}{2}$ cup honey,
$\frac{1}{4}$ cup soft butter,
$\frac{1}{2}$ cup shredded coconut

Combine over low heat

$\frac{1}{2}$ cup honey,
$\frac{1}{4}$ cup butter,
1 Tbsp. lemon juice

Combine over low heat

2 ripe bananas, mashed,
1 Tbsp. lemon juice,
$\frac{1}{4}$ tsp. cinnamon,
$\frac{1}{2}$ cup honey

Combine over low heat

$\frac{1}{2}$ cup honey,
$\frac{1}{4}$ cup soft butter,
3 Tbsps. cocoa or carob

Combine over low heat

$\frac{1}{2}$ cup honey,
$\frac{1}{4}$ cup pureed fruit,
$\frac{1}{4}$ cup orange juice,
1 tsp. grated orange rind

Combine over low heat

$\frac{1}{2}$ cup honey,
$\frac{1}{4}$ cup butter,
handful of raisins,
$\frac{1}{4}$ tsp. ginger or cinnamon

UNCLE PAUL'S SILVER DOLLAR PANCAKES

Equipment:

large skillet or electric frying pan
2 mixing bowls
wire whisk (optional)
mixing spoon
measuring cup
measuring spoons
metal spatula

Ingredients:

1 cup whole-wheat or
   unbleached white flour
$\frac{1}{2}$ tsp. baking soda
$\frac{1}{2}$ tsp. salt
1 cup buttermilk
2 eggs
3 Tbsps. vegetable oil

Method:

1. Combine flour, baking soda, and salt in mixing bowl.
2. In separate mixing bowl, beat together buttermilk, eggs, and oil.
3. Add liquid ingredients to dry ingredients. Beat until all ingredients are moistened.
4. Drop batter by tablespoons onto hot, greased skillet. Cook both sides until brown.

JOHNNYCAKES

Equipment:

large skillet or electric frying pan
mixing bowl
wire whisk (optional)
mixing spoon
measuring cup
measuring spoons
metal spatula

Ingredients:

1 cup milk
2 eggs
1 Tbsp. honey
3 Tbsps. vegetable oil
$1\frac{1}{2}$ cups cornmeal
1 tsp. salt

Jim-Dandy Johnnycake Additions:

2 very ripe bananas, mashed
$\frac{1}{2}$ cup toasted wheat germ
1 10-ounce package of frozen strawberries, thawed
1 cup chopped peanuts

Method:

1. Beat milk, eggs, honey, and oil together in mixing bowl. Add cornmeal and salt and stir until all ingredients are moistened.
2. If you want, add one of the Jim-Dandy Additions.
3. Drop batter onto hot, greased skillet by large spoonfuls. Cook both sides until golden-brown.

The name Johnnycake comes from "journey cake," which was one of the breads early American settlers, traveling across the country, could easily prepare at wayside camps.

FRENCH TOAST

Equipment:

large skillet or electric frying pan
mixing bowl
wire whisk (optional)
mixing spoon
measuring cup
measuring spoons
metal spatula

Ingredients:

3 eggs
$\frac{1}{3}$ cup milk
$\frac{1}{4}$ tsp. salt
$\frac{1}{2}$ tsp. vanilla extract
2 Tbsps. butter
8–10 slices of bread, fresh or stale

For Fancy French Toast:

1 banana, mashed
3 Tbsps. wheat germ
2 Tbsps. sesame seeds
1 tsp. cinnamon
$\frac{1}{4}$ cup apple or peach butter

Method:

1. Break eggs into mixing bowl and beat them well.
2. Add milk, salt, and vanilla and mix thoroughly. If you want Fancy French Toast, add one or more of the ingredients listed above.
3. Put the butter in the skillet and spread it evenly with spatula.
4. Soak the bread in the batter and cook both sides on a hot skillet until crispy and golden-brown. Add more butter to skillet for each new batch of toast.

YOGURT WHOLEWHEAT PANCAKES

Equipment:

large skillet or electric frying pan
2 mixing bowls
wire whisk (optional)
mixing spoon
measuring cup
measuring spoons

Ingredients:

$1\frac{1}{2}$ cups whole-wheat flour
3 Tbsps. baking powder
$\frac{1}{2}$ tsp. salt
$1\frac{1}{2}$ cups yogurt
3 eggs
$1\frac{1}{2}$ Tbsps. honey
3 Tbsps. vegetable oil

Method:

1. Combine flour, baking powder, and salt in mixing bowl.
2. In separate mixing bowl, beat together yogurt, eggs, honey, and oil.
3. Add yogurt mixture to flour mixture and stir until all ingredients are moistened.
4. Drop batter by large spoonfuls onto hot, greased skillet. Cook both sides until brown.

Today's my mom's birthday so I'm bringing her breakfast in bed.

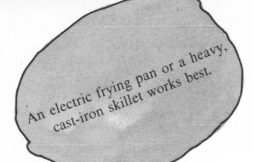

An electric frying pan or a heavy, cast-iron skillet works best.

Set temperature dial on electric frying pan to 380° or place skillet over medium heat and wait a few minutes until surface becomes very hot—you can tell it's ready when a few drops of cold water splashed on it bounce and then disappear. (If water just disappears without the bounce, the skillet is too hot.)

Flip the pancake when the edges have become firm and bubbles appear in the center. Cook the other side until well browned. These recipes make enough for four hungry people.

OATMEAL PANCAKES

Equipment:
large skillet or electric frying pan
2 mixing bowls
wire whisk (optional)
mixing spoon
measuring cup
measuring spoons
metal spatula

Ingredients:
$\frac{3}{4}$ cup whole-wheat or unbleached white flour
4 tsps. baking powder
$\frac{1}{2}$ tsp. salt
$1\frac{1}{2}$ cups uncooked oatmeal
2 eggs
1 Tbsp. vegetable oil
1 Tbsp. molasses
$1\frac{1}{4}$ cups milk

Method:
1. Combine flour, baking powder, and salt in mixing bowl.
2. Stir in the oatmeal.
3. In separate mixing bowl, beat together eggs, oil, molasses, and milk.
4. Pour egg mixture into flour mixture and stir until all ingredients are moistened.
5. Drop batter by large spoonfuls onto hot, greased skillet. Cook both sides until brown.

FILL 'EM & ROLL 'EM

TOP 'EM & EAT 'EM

BANANAS
WALNUTS
JAM
ALMONDS
RAISINS
PEANUT BUTTER

PLAIN OR FANCY PANCAKES

Equipment:

  large skillet or electric frying pan
  2 mixing bowls
  wire whisk (optional)
  mixing spoon
  measuring cup
  measuring spoons
  metal spatula

Ingredients:

  $1\frac{1}{2}$ cups whole-wheat flour or unbleached white
    flour
  $\frac{1}{4}$ tsp. salt
  2 tsps. baking powder
  $1\frac{1}{2}$ cups milk
  1 tsp. honey, molasses, or brown sugar
  2 eggs
  3 Tbsps. vegetable oil

For Fancy Pancakes:

  1 cup blueberries or sliced strawberries
  1 apple, grated, and 1 tsp. cinnamon
  1 cup chocolate chips
  1 cup chopped nuts and 1 tsp. cinnamon
  $\frac{1}{2}$ cup wheat berry or alfalfa sprouts
  2 carrots, grated
  $\frac{1}{2}$ cup shredded coconut

Method:

1. Combine flour, salt, and baking powder in mixing bowl. Blend thoroughly.
2. In separate mixing bowl, combine milk, honey, eggs, and vegetable oil. Beat well.
3. Add liquid ingredients to dry ingredients and stir until all ingredients are moistened.
4. If you want Fancy Pancakes, add one of the Fancy Ingredients listed above or make up your own.
5. Drop batter by large spoonfuls onto hot, greased skillet. Cook both sides until brown.

ignore the lumps in your pancake batter - they will cook out.

don't overbeat the pancake batter or they won't be as fluffy.

if the batter gets too thick, dilute it with milk, adding a little at a time.

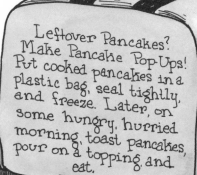

Leftover Pancakes? Make Pancake Pop-Ups! Put cooked pancakes in a plastic bag, seal tightly, and freeze. Later, on some hungry, hurried morning, toast pancakes, pour on a topping, and eat.

Some morning, pack one of these quick and easy Incredible Sandwiches, Creamy Dreamy Sandwich Spreads, or Bread Spreads in your lunchbox, and see what happens. You'll be the envy of the whole cafeteria and, who knows, maybe you'll be picked to pack your pack's picnic pack!

IT'S IN THE BAG

MAKING SCHOOL & PICNIC LUNCHES

THE INCREDIBLE SANDWICH LIST

Spread butter, mayonnaise, ketchup, mustard, relish, or anything else on any of the sandwiches at any time. Remember, this list is just a beginning. Soon you'll be thinking up your own incredible sandwich combinations. For more interesting sandwiches, use different kinds of bread:

BAGELS
BOSTON BROWN
CRACKED WHEAT
DATE NUT
DILL
FRENCH
OATMEAL
PUMPERNICKEL
RAISIN
RYE
SOUR DOUGH
SOY
SPROUTED RYE
SYRIAN
WHOLEWHEAT

If you don't know which Incredible Sandwich to choose, close your eyes and point.

· peanut butter & maple syrup ·
· peanut butter & honey & fresh fruit slices ·
· peanut butter & chopped nuts & banana slices ·
· peanut butter & bacon & tomato slices & lettuce ·
· peanut butter & cream cheese & jam & raisins ·
· peanut butter & dried fruit ·
· peanut butter & cucumber slices ·
· peanut butter & cream cheese & banana slices & raisins ·
· peanut butter & cream cheese & honey & cashews ·
· cream cheese & chopped dates ·
· cream cheese & fresh fruit slices & wheat germ ·
· cream cheese & dried apricots & chopped nuts ·
· cream cheese & dried fruit & cashews & sesame seeds ·
· cream cheese & grated carrots & raisins ·
· cream cheese & alfalfa or wheat sprouts & raisins ·
· cream cheese & leftover meat, chicken, or bacon ·
· cream cheese & cucumber slices & onion or radish slices ·
· cream cheese & olives & toasted sesame seeds ·
· cream cheese & pineapple slices & sunflower seeds ·
· cream cheese & shredded coconut & nuts ·
· cottage cheese & cucumber slices & fresh parsley & lettuce ·
· cottage cheese & apple slices & cinnamon ·
· cheese & tomato slices & lettuce & bean sprouts ·
· cheese & tomato slices & lettuce & toasted sesame seeds ·
· cheese & sliced apples ·

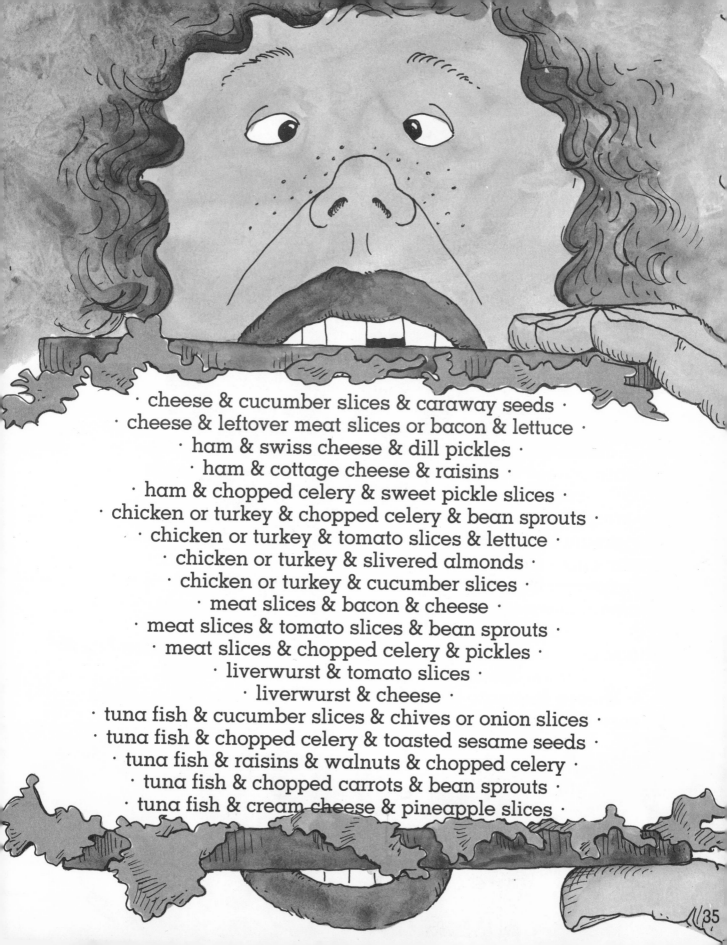

· cheese & cucumber slices & caraway seeds ·
· cheese & leftover meat slices or bacon & lettuce ·
· ham & swiss cheese & dill pickles ·
· ham & cottage cheese & raisins ·
· ham & chopped celery & sweet pickle slices ·
· chicken or turkey & chopped celery & bean sprouts ·
· chicken or turkey & tomato slices & lettuce ·
· chicken or turkey & slivered almonds ·
· chicken or turkey & cucumber slices ·
· meat slices & bacon & cheese ·
· meat slices & tomato slices & bean sprouts ·
· meat slices & chopped celery & pickles ·
· liverwurst & tomato slices ·
· liverwurst & cheese ·
· tuna fish & cucumber slices & chives or onion slices ·
· tuna fish & chopped celery & toasted sesame seeds ·
· tuna fish & raisins & walnuts & chopped celery ·
· tuna fish & chopped carrots & bean sprouts ·
· tuna fish & cream cheese & pineapple slices ·

MORE FOOD TO ADD TO THE
LUNCH BOX & PICNIC BASKET

- fresh fruit
  - fresh vegetable slices
- meat slices
  - dried fruit
  - olives & pickles
  - hard-boiled eggs
- hunk of cheese with crackers
- tub of cottage cheese or yogurt
  - roasted soybeans
- leftover drumsticks • popcorn
  - seeds • nuts
  - something to drink
...and don't forget something sweet

PRACTICAL POINTERS FOR PICNIC PACKERS

- Keep perishable picnic foods refrigerated from the moment you prepare them to the moment you leave.
- Tape the tops of containers that may come loose.
- Pack lettuce, tomatoes, and other juicy sandwich vegetables by themselves in separate plastic bags. Put them on your sandwich just before you eat.
- Avoid mayonnaise on warm days—it spoils quickly and makes sandwich bread soggy.
- Hot foods stay hot wrapped in aluminum foil. Cold foods stay cold wrapped in aluminum foil, and then wet newspaper. (If this gets messy, place it all in a paper- hot plastic-bag.)
- Ants are allergic to white chalk so to avoid them draw lines along the edges of the picnic table.

BREAD SPREADS

For other delicious nut butters use the same method with cashews, almonds, pecans, or any other nuts.

Change an ordinary sandwich with ordinary spread into an extraordinary experience by making the spread yourself! Homemade butter, peanut butter, and mayonnaise only take ten extra minutes to make, and beat anything you buy in the store.

For a different and delicious nut butter, add ¼ cup sunflower seeds or sesame seeds to peanuts.

For a chewier and sweeter nut butter, add ¼ cup raisins, dates, currants, or apricots to nuts.

For chunky nut butter, stir a handful of chopped nuts into the ground nut butter.

PEANUT BUTTER

Equipment:
electric blender
rubber spatula
measuring cup
measuring spoons
mixing bowl

Ingredients:
1 cup raw or toasted peanuts
2 Tbsps. vegetable oil
$\frac{1}{4}$ tsp. salt

Method:
1. Grind peanuts in blender until powdery.
2. Scrape peanuts into the bowl and add oil and salt. Stir everything until well blended.
3. Store peanut butter in refrigerator.

BUTTER

Equipment:

electric blender
rubber spatula
mixing bowl
mixing spoon
strainer

Ingredients:

at least ½ pint heavy cream, warmed to room
temperature
½ cup ice water, just in case
salt (optional)

Method:

1. Whip heavy cream in blender jar at medium speed.
2. After about 30 seconds, the cream will become very thick (this is whipped cream). If the blender blades do not seem to be cutting through the whipped cream (the cream will be motionless), remove the inner cap of blender top and add the ice water (without the ice). Keep blending.
3. After a minute or so, the thick cream will suddenly become thin. Thick, yellowish blobs will float to the top. These blobs are the butter, and the thin liquid beneath is buttermilk.
4. Draw off the buttermilk from the butter by pouring everything through the strainer. You may want to save the buttermilk for drinking or for cooking—it's great for pancakes (see Uncle Paul's Silver-Dollar Buttermilk Pancakes, page 28).
5. Put the butter in the bowl and work out the remaining buttermilk by mashing butter along sides of bowl with the spoon. Pour off buttermilk.
6. Add salt to taste, but if you want sweet butter, don't add any. Add any Better Butter Additions you'd like and store in a closed container in refrigerator.

BETTER BUTTER ADDITIONS:

1 Tbsp. chopped parsley

1 Tbsp. chives

1 tsp. dill

½ tsp. tarragon

1 tsp curry powder

½ tsp. dried mustard

1 Tbsp. grated cheese

2 tsp. orange or lemon rind, grated

1 Tbsp. catsup or chili sauce

1 clove garlic, crushed

ANOTHER WAY TO MAKE BUTTER:

And strong muscles!
Put the heavy cream in a jar, cover tightly,
and shake . . . and shake . . . and shake.
Keep shaking until the butter separates
and floats to the top.

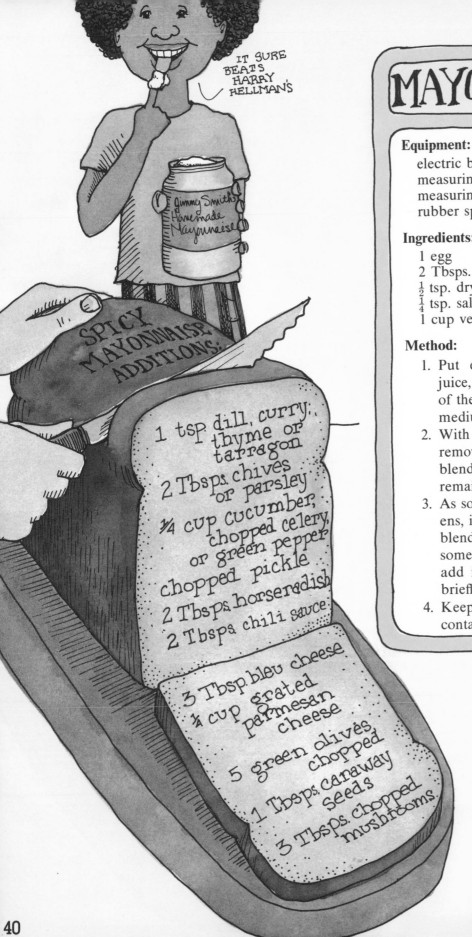

IT SURE BEATS HARRY HELLMAN'S

Jimmy Smith's Homemade Mayonnaise

SPICY MAYONNAISE ADDITIONS:

1 tsp. dill, curry, thyme or tarragon
2 Tbsps. chives or parsley
¼ cup cucumber, chopped celery, or green pepper
chopped pickle
2 Tbsps. horseradish
2 Tbsps. chili sauce

3 Tbsp. bleu cheese
¼ cup grated parmesan cheese
5 green olives chopped
1 Tbsps. caraway seeds
3 Tbsps. chopped mushrooms

MAYONNAISE

Equipment:
  electric blender
  measuring cup
  measuring spoons
  rubber spatula

Ingredients:
  1 egg
  2 Tbsps. vinegar or lemon juice
  ½ tsp. dry mustard
  ¼ tsp. salt
  1 cup vegetable oil

Method:
  1. Put egg, vinegar or lemon juice, mustard, salt, and ¼ cup of the oil in blender. Whiz at medium speed until mixed.
  2. With the blender still going, remove the inner cap from blender top and pour in the remaining ¾ cup oil.
  3. As soon as the mixture thickens, it's mayonnaise. Turn off blender. If you choose to add some spice to the mayonnaise, add it now and blend again briefly.
  4. Keep refrigerated in a closed container.

If you are substituting fresh herbs for dry, triple the amount. Dried herbs are 3 times more concentrated than fresh. Measurements in this book are for dry herbs.

YOGURT CHEESE IS ALSO GOOD AS A VEGETABLE DIP OR CRACKER SPREAD.

YOGURT CHEESE

Start this recipe the night before the day you want to eat it. It takes only 10 minutes of your time, but it has a lot of work to do on its own.

Equipment:

The night before:
small mixing bowl
large piece of cheesecloth, double thickness
rubber band

The morning after:
mixing bowl
mixing spoon
measuring spoons

Ingredients:

2 cups plain yogurt, your own or from the store

Method:

The night before:

1. Lay the cheesecloth across the mixing bowl and carefully pour the yogurt into the center.
2. Gather together the ends of the cheesecloth and secure them with the rubber band. Hang this bundle from the water faucet over the kitchen sink.

The morning after:

1. Remove the cheesecloth and you'll find a firm ball of yogurt cheese, very similar to cream cheese. All the liquid from the yogurt has drained through the cheesecloth, leaving only the creamy solids.
2. Eat the cheese as it is, or flavor it with one of the Tasty Yogurt Cheese Additions. Store in refrigerator.

If you lived in Lapland, your yogurt might be made from mare or reindeer's milk. If you lived in Armenia, you might eat yogurt made from buffalo or goat's milk. In this country don't worry—it's from cow's milk.

TASTY YOGURT CHEESE ADDITIONS: (add 1 or several)

salt and pepper
1 clove garlic, minced
1 Tbsp. chives or parsley
1/2 tsp. mint leaves or celery seed
1/4 tsp. curry powder
bean sprouts
chopped vegetables— onion, green pepper or celery
honey
raisins or nuts

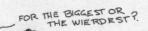

WE'RE TRYING TO GET INTO GUINNESS' BOOK OF WORLD RECORDS.

FOR THE BIGGEST OR THE WIERDEST?

I KNOW A GIANT WHO'D BE INTERESTED WHEN YOU'RE DONE.

CREAMY
DREAMY

Try one of these delicious Sandwich Spreads on a slice of fresh bread. They're so good your parents may ask you to ask them to lunch.

SANDWICH
SPREADS

I'VE GOT A DATE WITH A CASHEW

Absolutely heavenly on date nut, banana nut, or raisin bread. Don't miss it.

Equipment:
electric blender
rubber spatula
measuring cup
measuring spoons
small mixing bowl
fork

Ingredients:
1 cup unsalted cashews
2 Tbsps. vegetable oil
1 ripe banana
½ cup chopped dates

Method:
1. Grind cashews in blender on high speed until powdery.
2. Scrape cashews into the mixing bowl with spatula. Add vegetable oil and banana and mash everything together with the fork.
3. Add dates and stir well.

IF YOU HEAR OF ANYONE MAKING A BIGGER ONE, WILL YOU LET US KNOW?

A LITTLE HISTORY (never hurts):

According to legend, the sandwich was invented in England in the late 1700's, by the Fourth Earl of Sandwich. This gambling man once refused to leave the card table for over 24 hours. Ignoring calls to the dinner table, he ordered a servant to bring him meat placed between two slices of buttered bread and kept right on playing.

Deal 'em

BABOON BUTTER

A boon to any kind of bread, from cracked wheat to raisin.

Equipment:
mixing bowl
fork
measuring cup

Ingredients:
$\frac{1}{2}$ cup peanut butter
1 large or 2 small very ripe
  bananas
$\frac{1}{4}$ tsp. cinnamon
1 Tbsp. shredded coconut
handful of raisins, currants, or
  chopped dates

Method:
1. Mash together the peanut butter and bananas in mixing bowl with fork.
2. Add cinnamon, dried fruit, and coconut. Mash again until everything is well blended.

RAISINS IN THE SUN

Terrific on raisin, oatmeal, banana nut, or whole-wheat bread.

Equipment:
mixing bowl
fork
measuring cup
measuring spoons

Ingredients:
$\frac{1}{2}$ cup peanut butter
$\frac{1}{2}$ cup cream cheese
1 Tbsp. honey
$\frac{1}{4}$ cup raisins
1 heaping tsp. grated orange peel
  or 1 Tbsp. orange juice

Method:
1. Mash peanut butter and cream cheese together in mixing bowl with fork.
2. Add honey, raisins, and orange peel or juice. Mix well.

$\frac{1}{2}$ CUP HONEY
+ $\frac{1}{2}$ CUP BUTTER, SOFTENED
_____
1 CUP HONEY BUTTER

Now, take ½ cup honey butter, add 2 slices bread and one hungry person- what do you have?

one full person?

I love this new math

43

Keep a few onions in the refrigerator and cut them chilled. If you don't have time for that, peel them under cold running water.

MEDITERRANEAN MASH

This is a variation of the Middle Eastern dish "hummus." Traditionally served as a dip for bread, fish, or vegetables, a scoop on lettuce makes a fine salad or, with Syrian flatbread or a bagel, a tasty sandwich.

Equipment:
    electric blender
    rubber spatula
    measuring cup
    measuring spoons

Ingredients:
    1 cup cooked or canned garbanzo beans (also called chick-peas)
    juice of 1½ lemons
    ¼ cup tahini
    ½ tsp. salt
    1 small clove garlic, crushed

Method:
    Combine all ingredients in blender and whiz on medium speed until smooth. If mixture gets too thick, add a little water. (You can also mash everything together with a fork in a mixing bowl but it's a lot more work.)

SEA SPREAD

Swell on any kind of bread.

Equipment:
    mixing bowl
    fork
    measuring cup
    measuring spoons

Ingredients:
    1 7-ounce can tuna, drained
    ½ cup sour cream
    1 small onion, finely chopped
    1 cup peeled and chopped cucumber
    1 Tbsp. lemon juice
    ¼ tsp. salt
    1 Tbsp. sweet relish or chopped sweet pickles
    generous dash of pepper

Method:
    Combine all ingredients together in mixing bowl and mash with fork until mushy.

WHEN EVERYHING ELSE FAILS...

TRY A ...LEMON

FOR SEASICKNESS: As soon as you begin to feel queasy, such a lemon.

FOR POISON IVY: Wash first and pat dry. Then apply lemon juice generously. Repeat if necessary.

FOR SORE THROAT: dilute lemon juice with water and gargle frequently

FOR OILY SKIN: Wash your face with lemon juice every night and leave on until morning.

FOR STAINED HANDS: Rub your hands well with lemon juice.

FOR WARTS: Soak the inner rind of lemon in vinegar for 24 hours. Apply to wart for 1 or 2 hours. Repeat with fresh lemon daily.

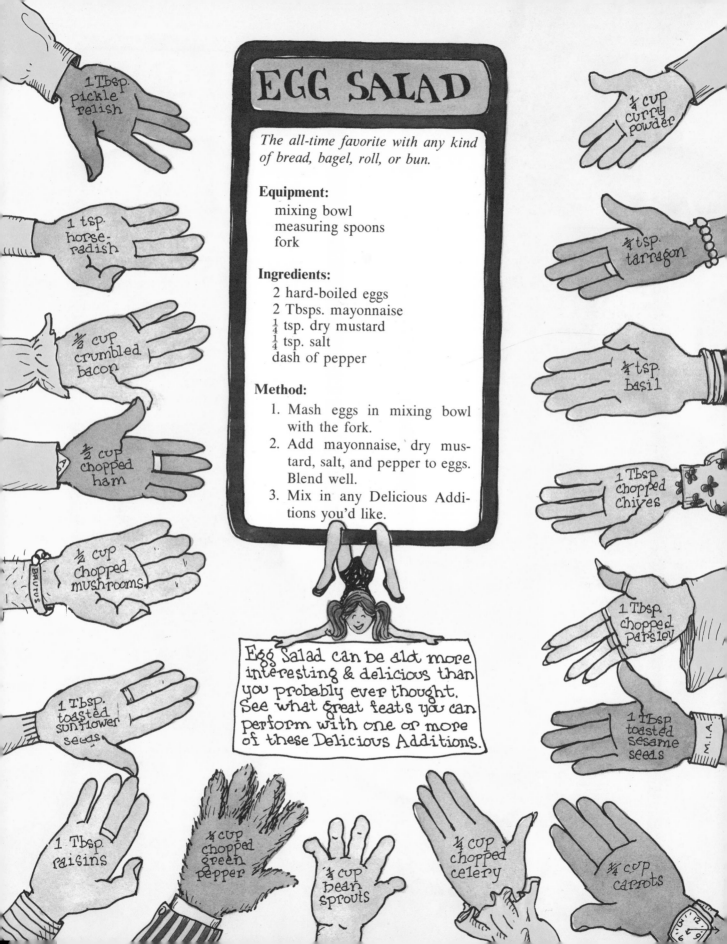

CRISP GARDEN SPREAD

Great on Syrian flatbread, toasted sprouted wheat, rye, or whole-wheat bread. Also makes a savory salad for dinner, or a dip!

Equipment:
mixing spoon
mixing bowl
rubber spatula
measuring cup
measuring spoons

Ingredients:
1 cup small-curd cottage cheese
$\frac{1}{4}$ cup mayonnaise
1 cup chopped cucumber (about $\frac{1}{2}$ medium cucumber)
1 tsp. dill
·salt and pepper

Method:
For sandwich and salad: Combine all ingredients in a mixing bowl and stir until blended. This sandwich is a little goopy, so wrap it in a plastic bag or wax paper.
For vegetable dip: Combine all the ingredients in the electric blender, and blend at medium speed.

GUACAMOLE

A traditional Mexican dip, delicious stuffed into Syrian flatbread.

Equipment:
mixing bowl
measuring cup
measuring spoons
mixing spoon

Ingredients:
1 ripe avocado
1 ripe tomato, chopped
$\frac{1}{4}$ cup mayonnaise
1 tsp. lemon juice
salt and pepper

Method:
1. Cut avocado in half lengthwise. Remove pit. Scoop out pulp and chop into little chunks.
2. Add chopped tomato, mayonnaise, lemon juice, salt and pepper. Stir until thoroughly mixed.

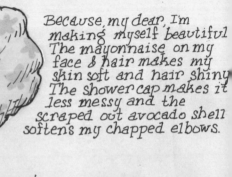

Because, my dear, I'm making myself beautiful. The mayonnaise on my face & hair makes my skin soft and hair shiny. The shower cap makes it less messy and the scraped out avocado shell softens my chapped elbows.

Mom! Why do you look so funny and smell like a salad and have green elbows?

EEEUUUU lieGUSTingll!

46

Have you ever wondered where the word BARBECUE comes from? (you haven't?) The story is that stranded pirates who were living on wild goat's meat invented a spicy sauce to baste the meat while they cooked it over an open fire. They were eaten "de barbe en queue", which in French means "from beard to tail". Personally, I try to avoid pirates. They really get my goat.

3 CHEESE BREEZE

Try this with pumpernickel, whole-wheat, dill, or rye bread.

Equipment:

  cheese grater
  mixing bowl
  measuring cup
  measuring spoons
  fork

Ingredients:

  $\frac{1}{2}$ cup cottage cheese
  2 Tbsps. cream cheese
  $\frac{1}{2}$ cup grated hard cheese—
    cheddar, colby, Swiss
  1 tsp. chopped chives or 1 clove
    garlic, minced (optional)
  $\frac{1}{4}$ tsp. salt

Method:

  1. Mash together the cottage cheese and cream cheese with fork.
  2. Add grated hard cheese, chives, garlic, and salt. Stir until thoroughly mixed.

A BARBECUE ON BREAD

A great bean sauce for toasted hamburger buns or hot-dog rolls.

Equipment:

  mixing bowl
  fork
  measuring cup

Ingredients:

  $\frac{1}{2}$ cup baked beans (or 1 9-ounce
    can, well drained)
  1 3-ounce package cream cheese
  handful of crumbled bacon or
    chopped ham
  $\frac{1}{4}$ tsp. salt
  generous dash of freshly ground
    pepper

Method:

  1. Mash baked beans and cream cheese together in mixing bowl with fork.
  2. Add bacon or ham, salt, and pepper. Mix well.

If you are having problems with vampires, hang a bulb of garlic over your bed and they will leave you alone at night.

SPROUTS

A GARDEN OF DELIGHTS

ONE WAY TO HELP YOURSELF REMEMBER TO RINSE YOUR SPROUTS IS TO MAKE A BIG, COLORFUL SIGN AND TAPE IT IN A PLACE YOU'LL BE SURE TO SEE IT. TAKE IT DOWN BETWEEN CROPS

Equipment:

very clean glass jar
cheesecloth or clean nylon stocking
rubber band
deep mixing bowl

Ingredients:

1 of these:
1 Tbsp. seeds—sesame, sunflower, or alfalfa
$\frac{1}{4}$ cup whole grains—wheat berry or rye
$\frac{1}{4}$ cup dried beans—mung beans (used in Chinese food), lentils, or soybeans

Method:

1. Use only clean, whole seeds, grains, or beans. Remove any that are broken and get rid of any debris.
2. Put seeds, grains, or beans in glass jar and fill with water. Cover mouth of jar with the piece of cheesecloth and secure it with the rubber band. Let them soak overnight.
3. Next morning, drain out the water and rinse sprouts in fresh water. Drain again.
4. Set jar mouth down in the mixing bowl and lean jar on a 45° angle. Keep bowl in a warm, dark place like a kitchen cupboard, or cover with a heavy towel.
5. Rinse sprouts and drain well twice a day, morning and evening. Don't forget!
6. Your sprouts will be ready to eat in 2 to 4 days. Just be sure to wait long enough for those long, white tails. Store in a closed container in refrigerator.

If you like Chinese food, you'll already know about bean sprouts—those crisp and delicious vegetables with the long tails. Bean sprouts are really the tiny beginnings of bean plants, and they combine a crunchy taste with many vitamins, minerals, and protein. It's simple to sprout your own kitchen garden with fresh beans, seeds, and grains.

Alfalfa Sprouts are ready when between 1 and 2 inches long They last several weeks in the refrigerator.

Mung Bean sprouts are best when between 2 or 3 inches long They sprout easily and are a good kind to begin with. Their taste is fresh & crunchy.

Wheatberries are best when between 1 to 2 inches in length. They are sweet and nutty tasting.

Soy Beans are a little more difficult to sprout. It is best to change their soaking water several times.

REMEMBER! Drain your sprouts very well or they can ferment and rot. Rotten sprouts taste rotten.

REMEMBER! Don't let your sprouts dry out. Rinse them at least twice a day in warm water. Cold water will retard growth.

REMEMBER! Keep your sprouts in a dark place. If sprouted in sunlight they turn brown and lose flavor.

REMEMBER Use a large jar. Beans and seeds expand quite a bit.

Sprouts have many uses besides in Chinese dinners. They can be added to sandwiches, tossed into salads, stirred into soups, scrambled into eggs, baked into bread, blended into pancake batter, or eaten by themselves.

Recipes in this book using sprouts: Scrambled Eggs, Omelet, Egg Salad, Yogurt Cheese, S.S. Celery, Munchable Mungs, Plain or Fancy Pancakes, Cream Cheese Balls

Don't be discouraged if a batch doesn't sprout. Follow the directions and keep trying until you're successful.

49

SNACKS IN A SNAP

If you're starved after school and dinner is years away, make the most of snack time by making the most of your new talents in the kitchen. These fast snacks take no baking, and you'll want to try all of them. But not all at once!

MAKING YOUR OWN SNACKS

SWEET SNACKS

BANANA SPLAT

Put a ripe banana into a bowl, mash it with a fork, and add any or all of the following: raisins, shredded coconut, chopped nuts, and chocolate syrup.

Just because something is sweet doesn't mean that it's not healthy. These recipes make some of the sweetest, best-tasting, and really good-for-you foods imaginable. Get ready for some lip-smacking snacking.

ANYDAY YOGURT SUNDAE

To a bowl of plain yogurt, add some applesauce or fruit preserves, raisins, chopped nuts, and shredded coconut.

STUFFED DATES

Remove the pits from a handful of dried dates and stuff them with dabs of cream cheese.

CRACKER SMACKS

Take 2 cookies or crackers and spread 1 with either jelly, honey, or mashed banana. Spread the other with either cream cheese, peanut butter, or other nut butter. Put them together and snack.

BANANAS FLOAT

Slice a banana into a bowl and cover with orange juice.

TOAST WITH THE MOST

Combine honey, carob or cocoa powder, and a dash of cinnamon. Spread this yummy spread on toast.

CHOCOLATE CRUNCHOLA

Equipment:
mixing bowl
fork
measuring cup
measuring spoons

Ingredients:
$\frac{1}{2}$ cup peanut butter
$\frac{1}{4}$ cup ($\frac{1}{2}$ stick) butter, softened
1 cup granola or oatmeal
$\frac{1}{2}$ cup chocolate chips
$\frac{1}{2}$ cup raisins
$\frac{1}{4}$ tsp. vanilla extract
$\frac{1}{4}$ cup shredded coconut

Method:
1. Mash peanut butter and butter together in mixing bowl with fork.
2. Stir in granola or oatmeal, chocolate chips, raisins, and vanilla. Blend thoroughly.
3. Roll into bite-sized balls and coat with shredded coconut.
4. Store leftover Crunchola in refrigerator.

51

BANANA SMASH

Equipment:
 mixing bowl
 fork
 measuring cup
 measuring spoons
 rubber spatula
 pie plate

Ingredients:
 2 very ripe bananas
 1 3-ounce package cream cheese
 $\frac{1}{4}$ cup ($\frac{1}{2}$ stick) butter, softened
 2 Tbsps. carob powder or cocoa
 1 cup chopped nuts
 $\frac{1}{2}$ cup shredded coconut
 1 Tbsp. honey or maple syrup
 $1\frac{1}{2}$ cups rice cereal

Method:
1. Smash bananas in mixing bowl with fork until mushy.
2. Add cream cheese and butter and smash with bananas.
3. Stir in carob or cocoa, nuts, coconut, and honey until mixture is well blended.
4. Add rice cereal and mix well.
5. Pour mixture onto plate and, using the spatula, spread it out evenly to the edges.
6. You can bite into it now, but for chilling thrills, or thrilling chills, place plate in the freezer and let Smash harden (about 2 hours). Cut into squares when ready to eat.

POP DROPS

Equipment:
 mixing bowl
 mixing spoon
 measuring cup
 double boiler
 rubber spatula
 greased cookie sheet

Ingredients:
 1 cup freshly popped popcorn
 1 cup chopped nuts—peanuts are perfect
 $\frac{1}{2}$ cup raisins
 1 cup (16-ounce package) chocolate chips

Method:
1. Combine popcorn, chopped nuts, and raisins in mixing bowl.
2. Heat the chocolate chips in top half of the double boiler until they have completely melted.
3. Scrape out melted chocolate with the rubber spatula and pour it into the mixing bowl with the popcorn, nuts, and raisins.
4. Stir mixture until the popcorn, peanuts, and raisins are completely chocolate coated.
5. Drop mixture by small spoonfuls onto cookie sheet. After chocolate has cooled, Pop Drops are ready to be popped in your mouth (and Pop Drops are popular with pops, too!). Store in a cool place.

Bananas are ripe when completely yellow & flecked with brown. Ripen your bananas at room temperature and store them in the refrigerator. This will turn the skin black but keep the inside fresh longer.

peel it first, you banana!

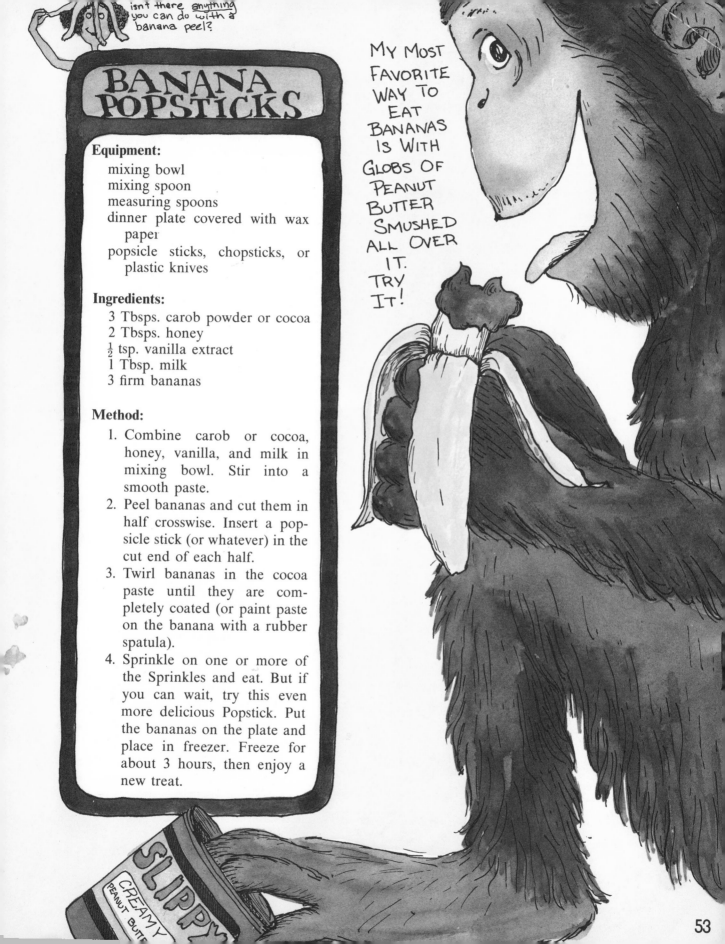

isn't there anything you can do with a banana peel?

BANANA POPSTICKS

Equipment:

mixing bowl
mixing spoon
measuring spoons
dinner plate covered with wax paper
popsicle sticks, chopsticks, or plastic knives

Ingredients:

3 Tbsps. carob powder or cocoa
2 Tbsps. honey
$\frac{1}{2}$ tsp. vanilla extract
1 Tbsp. milk
3 firm bananas

Method:

1. Combine carob or cocoa, honey, vanilla, and milk in mixing bowl. Stir into a smooth paste.
2. Peel bananas and cut them in half crosswise. Insert a popsicle stick (or whatever) in the cut end of each half.
3. Twirl bananas in the cocoa paste until they are completely coated (or paint paste on the banana with a rubber spatula).
4. Sprinkle on one or more of the Sprinkles and eat. But if you can wait, try this even more delicious Popstick. Put the bananas on the plate and place in freezer. Freeze for about 3 hours, then enjoy a new treat.

MY MOST FAVORITE WAY TO EAT BANANAS IS WITH GLOBS OF PEANUT BUTTER SMUSHED ALL OVER IT. TRY IT!

SLIPPY
CREAMY
PEANUT BUTTER

PEANUT BRITTLE

Because of the large amounts of brown sugar, this snack can't claim to be as healthy as the others, but it's so much fun to make and eat that it had to be included.

Equipment:
- small, heavy skillet
- wooden mixing spoon
- measuring cup
- rubber spatula
- greased dinner-size plate

Ingredients:
- 1 cup brown sugar
- 1 cup peanuts

Method:
1. Measure peanuts and place them on the counter near stove.
2. Put brown sugar in skillet and place over *low* heat.
3. Stir constantly with the flat side of mixing spoon until sugar has completely melted. (It will be the consistency of hot fudge sauce.)
4. Immediately remove skillet from heat and stir in peanuts. Work quickly because the sugar begins to harden right away.
5. Scrape out mixture with the rubber spatula and pour it onto the greased plate.
6. As soon as the Brittle has cooled, it's ready to eat. Break it into pieces and crunch. Leftovers can be placed in a pretty dish and left where the rest of the family can discover them.

Peanuts are not really nuts at all. They are legumes, the same as peas and beans.

Peanuts are sometimes called "Nature's Food Masterpiece" because of their large amount of protein, vitamins and minerals (and their good taste).

Another name for peanut is goober.

The Indians were raising peanuts in Virginia when the first settlers came. The peanut plant was one of their first gifts to white men.

One pound of peanut butter contains more protein than one pound of steak.

Can you imagine a ballgame or a circus without peanuts?

Nothing is wasted in a peanut plant—the vines, shells & skins are all used to feed livestock.

Peanuts grow under ground, as shown here. Luckily, worms don't like them.

PEANUT BUTTER POCKETS

Equipment:
- mixing bowl
- mixing spoon
- measuring cup
- cookie sheet

Ingredients:
- 1 cup peanut butter
- 1 cup dry milk powder
- $\frac{1}{2}$ cup honey
- $\frac{1}{4}$ cup toasted wheat germ

Pocket Fillings:
- whole nuts
- chocolate chips
- raisins
- strawberries
- jam or jelly

Method:
1. Combine peanut butter and dry milk powder in mixing bowl. Blend thoroughly.
2. Add honey and wheat germ and stir until the batter is smooth.
3. Drop the peanut butter mixture by tablespoons onto the cookie sheet. Press into patties about 3 inches wide.
4. Pick a Pocket Filling and place in the center of each. Fold the sides of the peanut butter patty around the filling to form a ball.
5. Store Peanut Butter Pockets in refrigerator, not in your pockets.

Dr. George Washington Carver, the son of slaves, spent 50 years studying the peanut. He discovered over 300 uses for them, including soap, ink, dye, linoleum, face cream and, best of all, butter.

BETTER PEANUT BUTTER BATTER BALLS

Equipment:
- mixing bowl
- mixing spoon
- measuring cup
- measuring spoons

Ingredients:
- 1 cup crunchy peanut butter
- $\frac{1}{2}$ cup dry milk powder
- 1 cup shredded coconut
- $\frac{1}{4}$ tsp. almond extract or 1 tsp. vanilla extract
- 1 cup chopped dates
- $\frac{1}{4}$ cup toasted sesame seeds

Method:
1. Combine peanut butter and dry milk powder in mixing bowl.
2. Stir in coconut, extract, and chopped dates. Blend thoroughly.
3. Roll mixture into bite-sized balls and coat with toasted sesame seeds.
4. Store BPBBBs in refrigerator.

NUT BRITTLE

In place of peanuts, use 1 cup chopped nuts, any kind you want. How about Walnut Brittle or Pecan Brittle?

SESAME SWEET

In place of peanuts in the Peanut Brittle recipe, use $\frac{1}{2}$ cup sesame seeds.

APRICOT CREAM SUPREME

Equipment:

small saucepan with cover
mixing bowl
rubber spatula
fork
measuring cup
measuring spoons
strainer
pie plate

Ingredients:

1 cup water
½ cup chopped dried apricots
1 8-ounce package cream cheese
½ cup (1 stick) butter, softened
2 Tbsps. carob powder or cocoa
⅓ cup honey or maple syrup
½ cup chopped nuts—any kind
1 tsp. cinnamon

Method:

1. Pour water into saucepan and bring to a boil. Add apricots, return water to a boil, cover pan, and turn off heat.
2. In mixing bowl, mash together the cream cheese and butter with a fork until thoroughly blended.
3. Stir in carob or cocoa, honey, nuts, and cinnamon.
4. Drain off water from apricots and stir them into rest of ingredients in the mixing bowl.
5. Pour mixture into the pie plate and, if you can resist eating right away, refrigerate. If you can't resist, try spooning some on top of ice cream, or straight into your mouth.
6. When chilled, cut into small squares and serve. Dynamite! Leftovers should be stored in the refrigerator.

TO PEEL ALMONDS: Drop the nuts into a saucepan of boiling water. Let them boil for 1 minute. Drain and rinse them under cold water. Then pinch each nut between your thumb and pointer finger. Be careful—they can really fly!

TO SOFTEN HARD BUTTER QUICKLY: Find a bowl a little larger than the butter dish and fill it with boiling or very hot water. Let it stand a minute, pour the water out and place the bowl over the butter. Wait a few minutes, and your butter will be nicely softened. If it is still too hard, try it one or two more times.

DATE DROPS

Equipment:
- electric blender
- rubber spatula
- small mixing bowl
- measuring cup
- measuring spoons
- medium saucepan with lid

Ingredients:
- $\frac{1}{4}$ cup water
- $\frac{1}{2}$ tsp. cinnamon
- 1 8-ounce package chopped dates
- handful of whole almonds

Goodies:
- poppy seeds
- toasted sesame seeds
- toasted wheat germ
- shredded coconut
- ground nuts
- uncooked oatmeal

Method:
1. Put water and cinnamon in saucepan, set over high heat, and bring to a boil.
2. As soon as the water boils, add dates, cover pan, and reduce heat.
3. Simmer for 3 minutes. Turn off heat and let sit 5 minutes longer.
4. Pour date mixture into the electric blender jar and whiz on medium speed until smooth. Scrape date mixture into a bowl.
5. When dates have cooled, press a spoonful of the mixture around each almond to form a small ball.
6. Coat balls in one, two, three, or *all* of the Goodies.
7. Store in refrigerator.

Moo Chew Molasses are my favorite

MOO CHEW MOLASSES

Equipment:
- mixing bowl
- fork
- measuring cups
- measuring spoons
- pie plate

Ingredients:
- 1 8-ounce package cream cheese
- $\frac{1}{2}$ cup dry milk powder
- $\frac{1}{2}$ cup toasted wheat germ
- $\frac{1}{2}$ cup molasses
- 1 tsp. vanilla extract
- $\frac{1}{2}$ cup peanuts
- $\frac{1}{2}$ cup chopped dried fruit
- 1 Tbsp. grated orange peel

Method:
1. Mash cream cheese and dry milk powder together in mixing bowl with fork.
2. Add wheat germ, a little at a time, until mixture is smooth.
3. Add molasses, vanilla, peanuts, dried fruit, and orange peel. Stir until blended thoroughly.
4. Drop Moo Chews by teaspoons onto the plate. Store leftovers in refrigerator.

There are many different flavors of honey, depending on the kind of flowers the bees fed on.

We really have a lot to thank bees for. They not only make honey for us, but in doing so, pollinate the flowers on fruit trees, fertilizing them to make fruit.

Generally, the darker the honey, the stronger the flavor and the richer in vitamins it will be.

For every pound of honey a bee makes from 50,000 to 8,000 trips and each trip may be as long as 1½ miles.

Equal parts of honey and lemon juice, mixed together, make a good, old-fashioned cough medicine.

An excellent remedy for a bee sting is a slice of onion placed over the puncture. This relieves the sting and reduces the swelling.

If your honey becomes crystallized in the jar, set it in a pan of very hot water. Keep it stored in a warm and dry place.

hi honey!

THE INCREDIBLE SHRINKING CHOCOLATE SNAKE

Once you taste this, you'll understand why it's called "shrinking"!

Equipment:
large mixing bowl
mixing spoon
measuring cup
measuring spoons
clean hands
wax paper

Ingredients:
½ cup peanut butter or tahini
½ cup dry milk powder
½ cup honey
1 heaping Tbsp. carob powder or cocoa
½ tsp. vanilla extract
¼ cup chopped nuts—pecans, walnuts, peanuts, or other
¼ cup raisins
¼ cup chopped dates
2 heaping Tbsps. shredded coconut

Method:
1. Combine peanut butter or tahini and dry milk powder in mixing bowl. Stir until thoroughly blended.
2. Stir in, one at a time, honey, carob or cocoa, vanilla, nuts, raisins, dates, and coconut. Clean hands or a wooden spoon work best for this.
3. Put mixture on wax paper and roll into the shape of a fat snake. Pull or cut off pieces—they're ready to eat.
4. Wrap Rapidly Shrinking Snake in wax paper and store in refrigerator.

CREAM CHEESE BALLS WITH WHISKERS

Equipment:

mixing bowl
fork
measuring cup
measuring spoons

Ingredients:

1 8-ounce package cream cheese
2 Tbsps. honey or maple syrup
$\frac{1}{2}$ cup alfalfa or wheat sprouts
$\frac{1}{3}$ cup raisins or currants
$\frac{1}{3}$ cup chopped nuts
$\frac{1}{4}$ tsp. nutmeg
$\frac{1}{4}$ cup poppy seeds

Method:

1. Mash together cream cheese and honey or maple syrup in mixing bowl with fork.
2. Add, one at a time, sprouts, dried fruit, nuts, and nutmeg until completely blended with cream cheese.
3. Roll cream-cheese mixture into bite-size balls and coat with poppy seeds.
4. Store leftover Cheese Balls in refrigerator.

SWEET SESAME SQUISH

Equipment:

mixing bowl
measuring cup
measuring spoons
mixing spoon
wax paper
clean hands

Ingredients:

$\frac{1}{4}$ cup tahini
1 cup dry milk powder
$\frac{1}{2}$ cup honey
$\frac{1}{2}$ tsp. vanilla extract
$\frac{1}{4}$ cup chopped dried fruit
$\frac{1}{2}$ cup shredded coconut

Method:

1. Combine tahini and dry milk powder in mixing bowl. Stir until blended.
2. Add honey, vanilla, dried fruit, and coconut. Squish until mixed—clean hands work best for this.
3. Put mixture on wax paper and roll into a long, round log. Pull off a piece and eat.
4. Wrap the remaining Squish in wax paper and store in refrigerator.

White sugar has been found to be the best cure for hiccups. Take 1 tsp. by itself. But try not to get hiccups too often. White sugar contributes nothing to the body but calories & cavities.

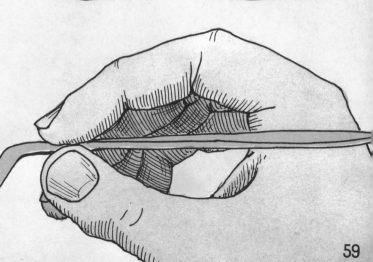

CRUNCHY

SWEET NUTS

Equipment:

- small, heavy skillet
- small mixing bowl
- measuring cup
- measuring spoons
- mixing spoon
- rubber spatula

Ingredients:

- 1 cup raw, unsalted walnuts, pecans, peanuts, or almonds
- 1 Tbsp. honey
- $\frac{1}{2}$ tsp. cinnamon
- dash of salt

Method:

1. Mix honey, cinnamon, and salt together in mixing bowl.
2. Add nuts and stir until they're thoroughly coated with honey mixture.
3. Scrape nuts into the frying pan and cook over low heat, stirring constantly, until nuts begin to brown.
4. Remove skillet from heat and scrape nuts into serving bowl. Let nuts cool before you sample them or your tongue will be sorry.

HOT NUTS

Equipment:

- small, heavy skillet
- measuring cup
- measuring spoons
- mixing spoon
- paper towel

Ingredients:

- 1 cup raw, unsalted nuts—any one kind or a mixture of different kinds
- 1 Tbsp. butter
- 1 of these Spice Mixtures:
    - $\frac{1}{2}$ tsp. curry powder
    - $\frac{1}{2}$ tsp. salt
    - *or*
    - $\frac{1}{4}$ tsp. dry mustard
    - $\frac{1}{2}$ tsp. chili powder
    - $\frac{1}{2}$ tsp. salt
    - *or*
    - 1 tsp. soy sauce
    - $\frac{1}{2}$ tsp. ginger powder

Method:

1. Melt butter in skillet over low heat and stir in nuts.
2. Keep stirring nuts until they brown, but do not burn. This takes about 5 minutes.
3. Remove skillet from heat and drain nuts on the paper towel. Put the Hot Nuts in a serving bowl and toss them with one of the Spice Mixtures. Don't eat Hot Nuts immediately or you'll fry the insides of your mouth. Store in a closed jar, or put leftovers in a nut dish so that everybody can have a nibble.

I'm nuts about hot pecans

You're just plain nuts!

nuts?

POPCORN

Equipment:
large saucepan with tight-fitting lid
measuring cup
measuring spoon
large serving bowl

Ingredients:
$\frac{1}{4}$ cup popcorn kernels
2 Tbsps. vegetable oil

Method:
1. Heat oil in pan over medium heat until very hot.
2. Quickly add popcorn and cover. Shake pan several times so that kernels are well coated with the oil.
3. When corn begins to pop, shake pan back and forth steadily until popping stops.
4. Pour into serving bowl and sprinkle with salt.

FOR PEPPIER POPCORN POUR ON ONE OF THE FOLLOWING:

¼ STICK BUTTER

¼ STICK BUTTER & SOME FRESHLY GROUND PEPPER

¼ STICK BUTTER MELTED WITH 2 TBLSP. BROWN SUGAR & 1 TSP. CINNAMON

¼ STICK BUTTER MELTED WITH 1 CLOVE GARLIC

¼ STICK BUTTER MELTED WITH 1 TBLSP. LEMON JUICE

¼ STICK BUTTER & ¼ CUP GRATED CHEESE

¼ STICK BUTTER MELTED WITH 1 TBLSP. PEANUT BUTTER

Is unpopped popcorn a problem? That's a sign that the popcorn has dried out. You can restore the moisture either by freezing the kernels for 24 hours before popping the next batch or by soaking the kernels in cold water for 15 minutes before popping them. To prevent popcorn from drying out, store it in the refrigerator.

GOOP & GORP

These are great to take with you when hiking or biking (bowling or strolling) in plastic bags for quick energy snacks.

The ingredients are given but the amount is not— that's up to you. If you don't have all the ingredients, use what you do have, and add anything else you want.

GORP

sunflower seeds
pumpkin seeds
toasted sesame seeds
raisins or other chopped
    dried fruit
chocolate chips or
    M&M's
chopped nuts
shredded coconut

GOOP

granola or uncooked oatmeal
raisins or chopped dried fruit
chopped nuts
wheat germ
shredded coconut
honey or peanut butter

Method for Goop and Gorp:

Mix everything together
in a mixing bowl.

For Goop:

Add just enough honey or
peanut butter to roll the goop
into balls, any size you want.

it's really wise to make your own chips

HOMEMADE POTATO CHIPS

Equipment:

food grater or paring knife
medium skillet (about 8 inches in diameter)
tongs or fork
paper towels

Ingredients:

1 or 2 potatoes, scrubbed and unpeeled
vegetable oil
salt or garlic salt

Method:

1. Place skillet over medium heat and add vegetable oil to a depth of about $\frac{1}{3}$ to $\frac{1}{2}$ inch.
2. While oil is heating, slice potatoes in the long, horizontal slot of the food grater, or slice them as *thinly* as possible with the knife. The thinner the potatoes are sliced, the crispier they will be.
3. When oil is hot but not smoking, add some of the potato slices to the frying pan. Don't crowd too many in at one time.
4. Cook potatoes on both sides until the edges are golden-brown.
5. Remove chips and drain on a double layer of paper towels.
6. Place potato chips in a serving bowl and sprinkle with salt or garlic salt. If you're feeling adventurous, try adding a pinch of one of your favorite spices. Be the first in your group to taste Thyme, Dill, Sage, Chili, or Curry Potato Chips.

BANANA CHIPS

Follow the directions for Potato Chips, only substitute peeled, *green* bananas for the potatoes. Again, the thinner they're sliced, the crispier they'll be.

POPSICLES

Popsicles are not made in a snap—they take 3 to 4 hours—but if you make enough at one time, you'll have a snack ready for some other hungry, hot afternoon.

FROOSICLE

Equipment:

small paper cups and popsicle sticks, or plastic popsicle molds

Ingredients:

fruit juice, any kind—or a mixture of two or more kinds

Method:

1. Pour the juice into the cups or plastic molds and place them in the freezer.
2. *If using paper cups,* let the juice harden until it's very thick and slushy, and then stick a popsicle stick into the center of each cup.
3. Continue to freeze popsicles until they're completely hard. When you're ready to eat one, peel off the paper cup or hold the plastic mold under hot tap water to loosen the frozen juice from the container. Lift out the Froosicle and sickle your pop.

YO GOFROO SICLE

Equipment:

small paper cups and popsicle sticks, or plastic popsicle molds
mixing bowl
mixing spoon

Ingredients:

plain yogurt
frozen juice concentrate, any kind

Method:

1. Mix any amount of yogurt—the amount depends on how many popsicles you want to make—with any amount of frozen fruit concentrate—the amount depends on how sweet and fruity you want it to taste.
2. If you wish to add a Popsicle Put-In, combine it with the yogurt and juice concentrate and whiz in an electric blender.
3. Spoon the mixture into the paper cups or plastic molds and place them in the freezer.
4. *If using paper cups,* let the mixture harden until it's thick and slushy, and insert a popsicle stick in the center of each cup.
5. Continue to freeze popsicles until they're completely hard. When ready to eat, peel off the paper cup or hold the plastic mold under hot tap water to loosen the frozen yogurt from the container. Lift out the Yogofroosicle and slurp.

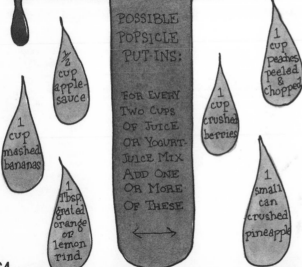

POSSIBLE POPSICLE PUT-INS:

FOR EVERY TWO CUPS OF JUICE OR YOGURT-JUICE MIX ADD ONE OR MORE OF THESE

½ cup applesauce

1 cup peaches peeled & chopped

1 cup mashed bananas

1 Tbsp grated orange or lemon rind

1 cup crushed berries

1 small can crushed pineapple

ROUND TIPPED BUTTER KNIVES OR TONGUE DEPRESSORS FROM YOUR DOCTOR CAN SUBSTITUTE FOR POPSICLE STICKS.

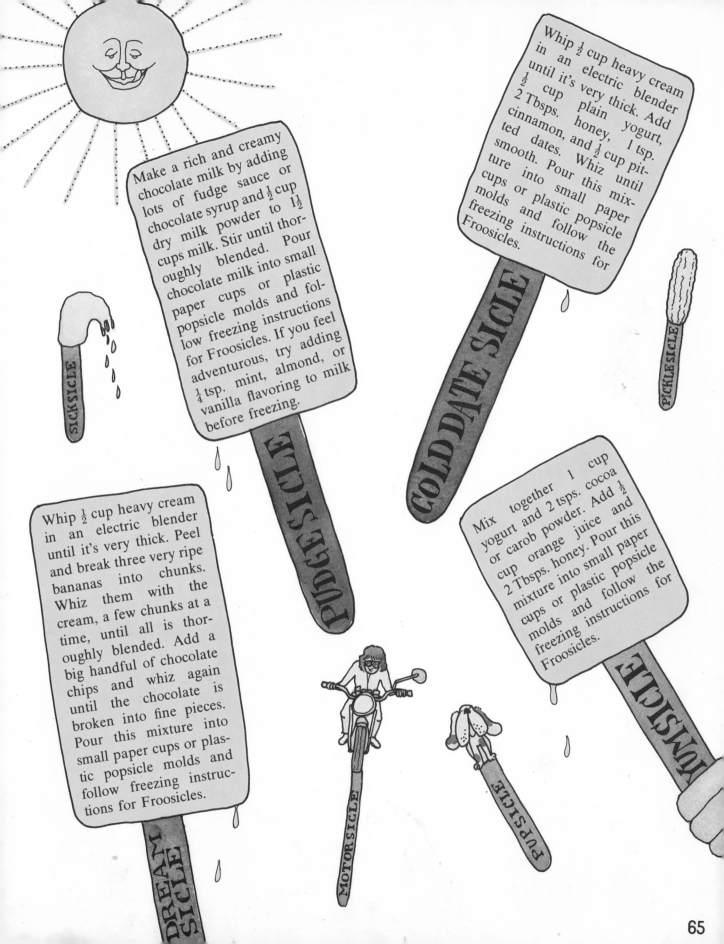

COLD DATE SICLE

Whip ½ cup heavy cream in an electric blender until it's very thick. Add ½ cup plain yogurt, 2 Tbsps. honey, 1 tsp. cinnamon, and ½ cup pitted dates. Whiz until smooth. Pour this mixture into small paper cups or plastic popsicle molds and follow freezing instructions for Froosicles.

SICKSICLE

PICKLESICLE

PUDGESICLE

Make a rich and creamy chocolate milk by adding lots of fudge sauce or chocolate syrup and ½ cup dry milk powder to 1½ cups milk. Stir until thoroughly blended. Pour chocolate milk into small paper cups or plastic popsicle molds and follow freezing instructions for Froosicles. If you feel adventurous, try adding ¼ tsp. mint, almond, or vanilla flavoring to milk before freezing.

DREAM SICLE

Whip ½ cup heavy cream in an electric blender until it's very thick. Peel and break three very ripe bananas into chunks. Whiz them with the cream, a few chunks at a time, until all is thoroughly blended. Add a big handful of chocolate chips and whiz again until the chocolate is broken into fine pieces. Pour this mixture into small paper cups or plastic popsicle molds and follow freezing instructions for Froosicles.

MOTORSICLE

PUPSICLE

YUMSICLE

Mix together 1 cup yogurt and 2 tsps. cocoa or carob powder. Add ½ cup orange juice and 2 Tbsps. honey. Pour this mixture into small paper cups or plastic popsicle molds and follow freezing instructions for Froosicles.

CRUNCHY CRACKER PUT-ONS

YUM

Mix and match ingredients from the two lists for a quicker cracker snack.

pepperoni slices	cucumber slices
ham slices	pickle slices
salami slices	pickle relish
cream cheese	olive slices
cottage cheese	chopped celery
peanut butter	crumbled bacon
cheddar (or other) cheese	bean sprouts

MMM WOW CRUNCHY CRACKER PUT-ONS

Send only $1 for FREE cookbook! "LOVE AT FIRST BITE"

NET WT. 454 GRAMS

CRUNCHY CRACKER SPREADS

THE WURST SPREAD

$\frac{1}{2}$ cup liverwurst
1 Tbsp. heavy cream, sour cream, or yogurt
something crunchy—pistachio nuts, toasted sunflower or sesame seeds

Mash together liverwurst and cream. Add crunchies and mix.

THE STICKIEST SPREAD

$\frac{1}{4}$ cup chunky peanut butter
2 Tbsps. tahini
1 tsp. honey
$\frac{1}{2}$ tsp. cinnamon

Mash together the peanut butter and tahini. Add the honey and cinnamon and mix.

THE CHEESIEST SPREAD

1 3-ounce package cream cheese
$\frac{1}{2}$ cup finely grated cheddar or colby cheese
$\frac{1}{4}$ tsp. Worcestershire sauce
few drops Tabasco
$\frac{1}{4}$ tsp. salt
$\frac{1}{4}$ cup finely chopped nuts

Mash together cream cheese and grated cheese. Add the rest of ingredients and mix together.

Fruits and vegetables don't belong just at meals—they're great snacks, too. Crisp and juicy, they help clean your teeth, keep you from getting fat, and are loaded with vitamins, minerals, and important enzymes.
And they taste terrific!

GARDEN SNACKS

THE MUNCHABLE MUNGS

Fill a small serving bowl with mung bean sprouts and season with salt and pepper. Now eat a handful of the nuttiest-tasting vegetables you've ever put in your mouth.

CUCUMBERSTICLE

Cut a cucumber in half across its width, peel one of the halves, and insert a popsicle stick in the flat end (a round-tipped knife or chopstick works well too). Squeeze on lemon juice and sprinkle with salt and maybe a little chili powder or dill. This is a favorite snack in Mexico.

THE CRUNCHY BUNCH

Clean a bunch of fresh raw vegetables . . . radishes . . . carrots . . . green beans . . . cucumbers . . . celery . . . cauliflower . . . green peppers . . . lettuce . . . zucchini . . . and cut them into bite-size pieces. Sprinkle them with salt or try one of the quick dips on the following pages.

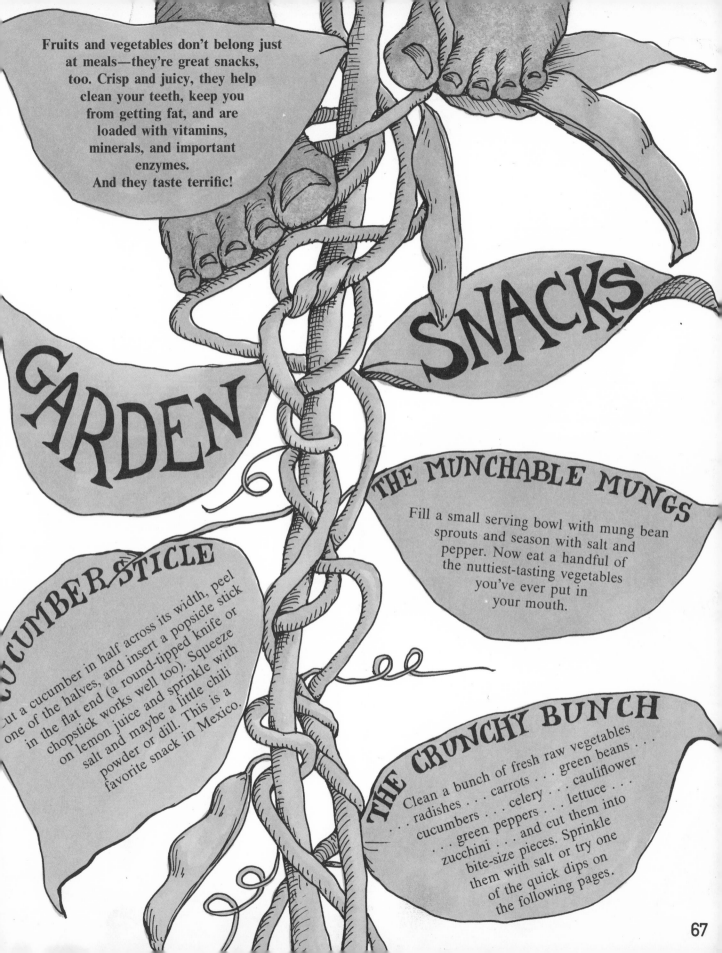

67

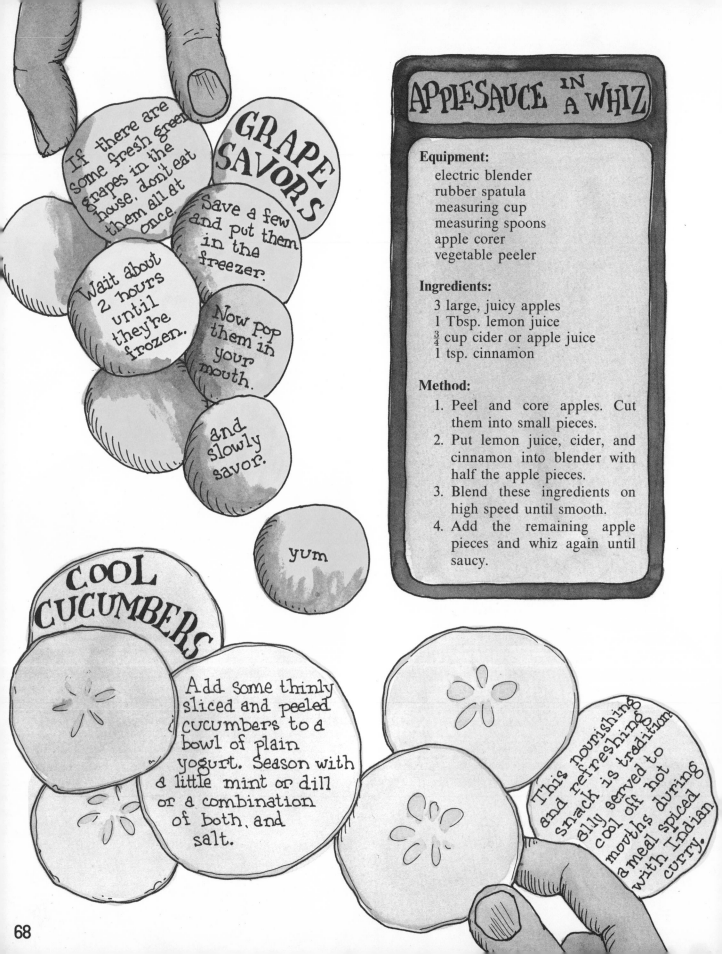

GRAPE SAVORS

If there are some fresh green grapes in the house, don't eat them all at once.

Save a few and put them in the freezer.

Wait about 2 hours until they're frozen.

Now pop them in your mouth.

and slowly savor.

yum

APPLESAUCE IN A WHIZ

Equipment:

electric blender
rubber spatula
measuring cup
measuring spoons
apple corer
vegetable peeler

Ingredients:

3 large, juicy apples
1 Tbsp. lemon juice
$\frac{3}{4}$ cup cider or apple juice
1 tsp. cinnamon

Method:

1. Peel and core apples. Cut them into small pieces.
2. Put lemon juice, cider, and cinnamon into blender with half the apple pieces.
3. Blend these ingredients on high speed until smooth.
4. Add the remaining apple pieces and whiz again until saucy.

COOL CUCUMBERS

Add some thinly sliced and peeled cucumbers to a bowl of plain yogurt. Season with a little mint or dill or a combination of both, and salt.

This nourishing and refreshing snack is traditionally served to cool off hot mouths during a meal spiced with hot Indian curry.

TOOTI-FROOTI IN A WHIZ

This is like applesauce, only you can choose the fruit flavor you favor.

Equipment:
- electric blender
- rubber spatula
- measuring cup
- measuring spoons
- vegetable peeler (for the fruits that need it)

Ingredients:
- 2 cups peeled and chopped fresh fruit—peaches, pears, berries, bananas, mangos, or other
- $\frac{1}{2}$ cup fruit juice—grape, apple, orange, cranberry, or other
- $\frac{1}{4}$ tsp. spice (optional)—cinnamon, allspice, or ginger

Method:
1. Put 1 cup fruit, fruit juice, and spice in blender jar and whiz until smooth.
2. Add the last cup of fruit pieces and blend again.

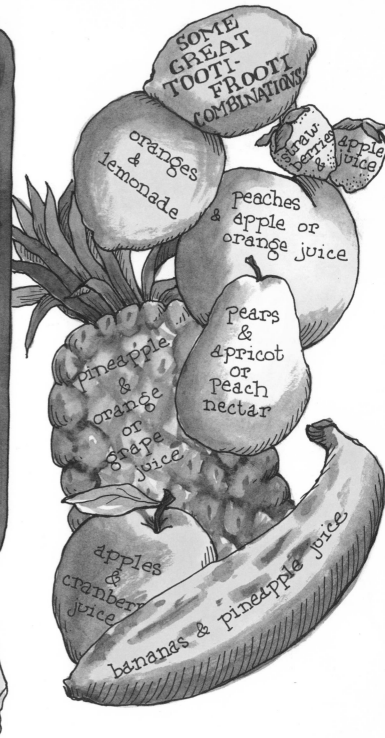

SOME GREAT TOOTI-FROOTI COMBINATIONS

oranges & lemonade

straw-berries & apple juice

peaches & apple or orange juice

pineapple & orange or grape juice

pears & apricot or peach nectar

apples & cranberry juice

bananas & pineapple juice

In the 1880's a young missionary, barefoot and dressed in a grain sack, set out for the wilderness of Ohio, Pennsylvania and and Indiana, where he roamed for the next 46 years, planting apple seeds so that the settlers who followed would have orchards. His name was John Chapman, but we know him as Johnny Appleseed. Quite a nice man.

A PRUNE IS JUST A DRIED-UP PLUM.

A RAISIN IS JUST A DRIED-UP GRAPE.

69

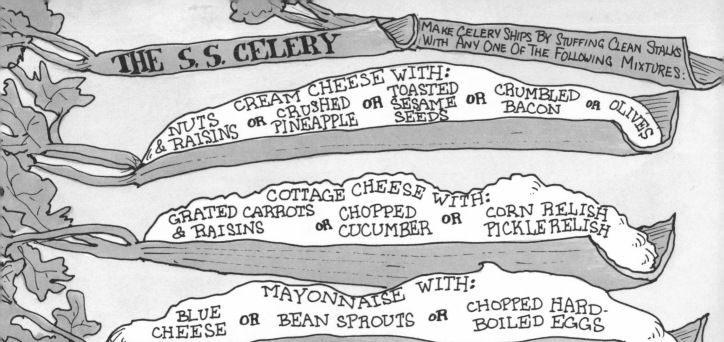

THE S.S. CELERY

MAKE CELERY SHIPS BY STUFFING CLEAN STALKS WITH ANY ONE OF THE FOLLOWING MIXTURES:

CREAM CHEESE WITH:
NUTS & RAISINS OR CRUSHED PINEAPPLE OR TOASTED SESAME SEEDS OR CRUMBLED BACON OR OLIVES

COTTAGE CHEESE WITH:
GRATED CARROTS & RAISINS OR CHOPPED CUCUMBER OR CORN RELISH PICKLE RELISH

MAYONNAISE WITH:
BLUE CHEESE OR BEAN SPROUTS OR CHOPPED HARD-BOILED EGGS

PEANUT BUTTER WITH:
ANYTHING YOU WANT

NIPPY DIP

Equipment:
small mixing bowl
mixing spoon
measuring cup
measuring spoons

Ingredients:
½ cup yogurt
2 heaping Tbsps. blue cheese
2 tsps. vinegar
1 tsp. dill

Method:
1. Combine all the ingredients in mixing bowl.
2. Mash the cheese along bottom and sides of bowl with mixing spoon until it is well blended with rest of ingredients.

CLAM DIP

Equipment:
mixing bowl
fork
measuring spoon

Ingredients:
1 7-ounce can minced clams
1 8-ounce package cream cheese
1 Tbsp. lemon juice
dash of pepper
salt to taste

Method:
1. Drain clams and save 1 Tbsp. of the juice.
2. Combine all the ingredients, plus reserved clam juice, in mixing bowl. Mash it all together with fork.

STALKING THE WILD MAYONNAISE

Equipment:

electric blender
rubber spatula
measuring cup
measuring spoons

Ingredients:

$\frac{1}{2}$ cup mayonnaise (try this with
the homemade kind, page 40)
1 cup chopped celery
1 Tbsp. chopped onion
$\frac{1}{2}$ tsp. salt
$\frac{1}{2}$ tsp. celery seeds

Method:

Combine all ingredients in
blender jar and whiz on high
speed until smooth. Green peppers, carrots, or cucumbers can
also be used instead of celery for
a yummy change.

Wilted vegetables can be restored by soaking them in
which 1 Tbsp. vinegar has been added. The cold water to
vinegar will not affect the taste.

GREEN CREAM DIP

Equipment:

electric blender (optional)
rubber spatula
measuring spoon
fork

Ingredients:

1 ripe avocado
1 Tbsp. sour cream
1 Tbsp. lemon juice
$\frac{1}{4}$ tsp. salt
1 clove garlic, crushed (optional)
1 tsp. caraway or dill seeds

Method:

1. Cut avocado lengthwise. Remove seed and scoop out pulp
   into blender jar. Whiz until
   creamy on medium speed.
2. Add the remaining ingredients and blend thoroughly.
   (You can also mash all the
   ingredients together in a mixing bowl with a fork or potato
   masher.)

To keep celery crisp,
store it in the refrigerator
in a jar or plastic bucket
with a few inches of
water in the bottom.

GETTING YOUR JUST DESSERTS

MAKING YOUR OWN SWEETS

How many dinners have you rushed through, hoping there would be a mouth-watering dessert at the end, only to be disappointed with what was (or wasn't) served? Now you can make sure that there will be a scrumptious dessert waiting for you and your family, too. Each recipe makes enough to serve four still-hungry people.

BOWL FOR ALL SEASONS

Fill a large serving bowl with at least 3 cups of sliced fresh fruit, as many different kinds as you want. Stir in 2 Tbsps. lemon juice. Dribble on honey or maple syrup and top off with a sprinkle of cinnamon, ginger, and shredded coconut.

SWEET & SOUR FRUIT

This is as delicious to eat as it is easy to make. Fill a serving bowl with about 3 cups sliced fresh fruit. (Melon balls, pineapple, strawberries, or green grapes are especially delicious.) Cover with sour cream and sprinkle generously with brown sugar.

MASTERPIECE MELON

Cut 2 small melons in half or 1 large melon in quarters (any kind except watermelon). Scoop out the seeds and fill the hole with a scoop of vanilla ice cream. Top with a big spoonful of berries— strawberries, blueberries, or raspberries.

FRUIT DESSERTS

TROPICAL TREASURE

Equipment:
- mixing bowl
- mixing spoon
- measuring cup
- serving bowl

Ingredients:
- 3 tangerines, peeled and sectioned, or 2 small cans mandarin oranges
- 1 small can crushed pineapple
- 2 bananas, sliced
- $\frac{1}{2}$ cup shredded coconut
- $\frac{1}{2}$ cup chopped nuts—walnuts, pecans, peanuts, or other
- 2 cups plain yogurt

Method:
1. Combine all ingredients in mixing bowl and stir well.
2. Pour into serving bowl and chill 2–3 hours in refrigerator before eating.

An easy way to remove the skin from citrus fruits: Put the fruit in a bowl, pour boiling water over it, and let it soak for 5 minutes. Cool under cold water, and pull the skin off.

YOGURT SLUSH SUNDAE

This is perfect to serve on a hot summer night—but start about 3 hours before dessert time.

Equipment:
- electric mixer (optional)
- mixing bowl
- mixing spoon
- measuring cup
- measuring spoons

Ingredients:
- 2 cups plain yogurt
- 1 6-ounce can frozen juice concentrate—grape, orange, lemonade, tangerine
- 1 tsp. crushed mint leaves or 3 sprigs fresh mint, finely chopped
- 2 cups chopped fruit, fresh or frozen

Method:
1. Beat together yogurt, frozen juice concentrate, and mint in mixing bowl until well mixed.
2. Place mixing bowl in freezer and chill until yogurt is slushy (about $1\frac{1}{2}$ hours).
3. Beat yogurt mixture again and return to freezer. It's ready to eat when firm.
4. Spoon Slush into individual bowls and top each serving with $\frac{1}{2}$ cup chopped fresh fruit.

YOGURT MUSH SUNDAE

Follow the directions above, but place all the ingredients, including the fruit, in the blender. Whiz at medium speed. Then proceed to Step 2.

SWEET SUMMER SOUP

Equipment:

electric blender
rubber spatula
chilled mixing bowl
mixing spoon
measuring cup
for peaches: medium saucepan, slotted spoon
for strawberries: strainer, small bowl

Ingredients:

6 peaches or 3 cups strawberries
½ cup honey
½ tsp. cinnamon
2 cups (1 pint) heavy cream

Method:

1. *For peaches:* Peel off the skins. An easy way to do this is to fill a medium saucepan halfway with water and bring to a boil. Immerse peaches in the boiling water and cook for no more than a minute. Remove them with the slotted spoon and stick them immediately under cold running water. Skins will peel off easily. Remove pits, cut peaches into small pieces, and combine with honey and cinnamon in blender jar. Whiz on high speed until smooth.
   For strawberries: Combine fruit, honey, and cinnamon in blender jar and whiz at high speed until smooth. Set strainer over small bowl and pour strawberry mixture into it. Mash the fruit along sides of strainer so that the juice and pulp are forced through. Throw remaining skins and seeds away.
2. *For peaches and strawberries:* Whip the heavy cream in the chilled mixing bowl until it stands in peaks.
3. Pour the fruit mixture into whipped cream and gently mix together.
4. Refrigerate several hours and serve with crisp cookies, if you have any. If not, it's tasty by itself.

CREAM WHIPS BEST IN A CHILLED BOWL.

To keep the bowl from slipping and sliding if you're whipping cream with an egg beater, place the bowl on a wet, folded cloth or towel.
Also, remember cream doubles in volume when whipped so use a large enough bowl.

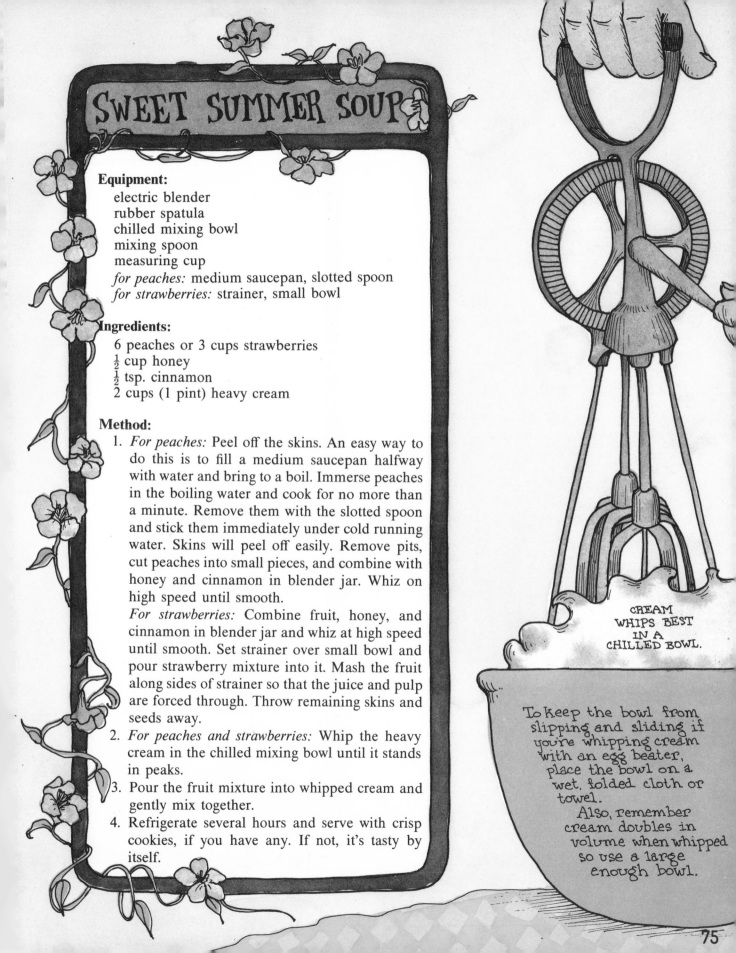

NO-BAKE BAKED GOODS

We are thankful to the Indians not only for this delicious recipe, but also for the cornmeal that goes into it. Corn, a difficult plant to grow, had been cultivated for many years by the Indians before European settlers came to America. When they did come, the Indians were able to teach them how to grow corn, using many of the methods we still use today. Corn became so important to the pioneers that they even used it to pay rent, taxes, and debts.

INDIAN PUDDING

This is a variation of the original recipe the Indians gave to early American settlers.

Equipment:
mixing bowl
mixing spoon
measuring cup
measuring spoons
double boiler
serving bowl

Ingredients:
2 cups milk
$\frac{1}{4}$ cup cornmeal
2 eggs, slightly beaten
2 Tbsps. molasses
$\frac{1}{4}$ cup brown sugar
$\frac{1}{2}$ tsp. ginger
1 tsp. cinnamon
pinch of powdered cloves
$\frac{1}{4}$ tsp. salt
$\frac{1}{2}$ tsp. vanilla extract
$\frac{1}{2}$ cup raisins

Method:
1. Put milk in top half of double boiler and stir in cornmeal, beaten eggs, molasses, and brown sugar.
2. Add ginger, cinnamon, cloves, and salt.
3. Stirring frequently, cook until mixture thickens (it should thicken like oatmeal). Remove pan from heat.
4. Add vanilla and raisins to the mixture and stir well.
5. Pour pudding into serving bowl. Serve with heavy cream, whipped cream, or ice cream.

BANANA CAKE

Equipment:

2 mixing bowls
electric blender
electric mixer (optional)
measuring cup
measuring spoons

mixing spoon
rubber spatula
bread pan
wax paper

Ingredients:

10 whole graham crackers
1 cup unsalted walnuts, almonds, or cashews
$\frac{1}{2}$ cup butter, melted
1 8-ounce package cream cheese
4 tsps. carob powder or cocoa
3 Tbsps. honey or maple syrup
1 tsp. cinnamon
4 cups thinly sliced bananas
1 large handful of shredded coconut

Method:

1. Crumble graham crackers (see Graham-Cracker Crust, page 78). Grind nuts in electric blender on medium speed until powdery.
2. Mix the graham crackers and nuts together—clean hands work very well for this—and add the melted butter. Mix again.
3. In a separate mixing bowl, mash the cream cheese, carob or cocoa, sweetener, and cinnamon. To make a really smooth mash, use the electric mixer.
4. Add the banana slices to the cream-cheese mash and gently stir with the mixing spoon until all the banana slices are coated.
5. Place a large piece of wax paper in the bread pan so that it extends over the sides. Put $\frac{1}{3}$ of the graham cracker crumbs on the bottom of the pan and then add $\frac{1}{3}$ of the banana slices. Carefully spread them over the length of the pan. Continue layering the crumbs and banana slices, ending with a layer of bananas on top.
6. Sprinkle the shredded coconut on top to decorate.
7. Refrigerate the cake for several hours. When you're ready to eat, remove the cake from the pan by lifting the wax paper and sliding it onto a pretty serving plate. Slice it as you would a loaf of bread.

LE BEST BROWN

HOW TO DEAL WITH BOULDERIZED BROWN SUGAR:

CLUNK

TO USE IMMEDIATELY:
Grate it on the large holes of a grater.

TO PREVENT HARDENING:
Store it in the refrigerator, tightly sealed.

TO SOFTEN:
Put sugar in a jar, add several slices of apple, cover tightly. Remove apple when the sugar is soft.

There are lots of beautiful ways to decorate pies with fruit or whipped cream. See how artistic you can be.

GRAHAM CRACKER PIE CRUST

Equipment:
electric blender, or sturdy bag and rolling pin
1 9-inch pie pan
mixing bowl
mixing spoon
measuring cup
measuring spoons
small saucepan

Ingredients:
10 whole graham crackers (or 30 hard cookies, like vanilla wafers or gingersnaps)
$\frac{1}{2}$ stick butter

Method:
1. Make crumbs by putting graham crackers or cookies in a sturdy bag (secure open end with a rubber band) and mashing with the rolling pin *or* by crumbling crackers in the electric blender and whizzing them on medium speed, a few at a time, until powdery.
2. Melt butter in saucepan over low heat.
3. Put crumbs in mixing bowl, pour on melted butter, and blend together. Clean hands work best for this.
4. Press the mixture evenly around the edges and bottom of the pie pan.
5. Fill with your favorite pie filling or try one of the following.

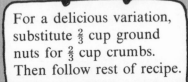

For a delicious variation, substitute $\frac{2}{3}$ cup ground nuts for $\frac{2}{3}$ cup crumbs. Then follow rest of recipe.

PUMPKIN PIE FILLING

This makes not only a superb pie filling, but also a delicious pudding, dished into individual serving bowls.

Equipment:
2 small mixing bowls
1 large mixing bowl
mixing spoon
measuring cup
measuring spoons
double boiler
eggbeater

Ingredients:
3 eggs, separated
$\frac{1}{3}$ cup honey or $\frac{2}{3}$ cup brown sugar
1 16-ounce can pumpkin
$\frac{1}{2}$ cup milk
$\frac{1}{2}$ tsp. salt
1 tsp. cinnamon $\quad \frac{1}{4}$ tsp. cloves
$\frac{1}{4}$ tsp. nutmeg $\quad \frac{1}{2}$ tsp. ginger
1 Tbsp. unflavored gelatin
$\frac{1}{4}$ cup cold water
2 Tbsps. honey

Method:
1. In large mixing bowl beat the egg yolks until thick. Add honey or brown sugar, pumpkin, milk, salt, cinnamon, nutmeg, cloves, and ginger. Mix well.
2. Cook pumpkin mixture on top of double boiler for 10 minutes, stirring occasionally.
3. In one small mixing bowl soften gelatin in cold water.
4. Remove double boiler from heat and add gelatin to pumpkin mixture.
5. In the other small bowl, beat egg whites until foamy. Dribble in the 2 Tbsps. honey and continue beating until stiff.
6. Add egg whites to pumpkin mixture and fold in gently.
7. Pour filling into pie crust and refrigerate several hours before serving.

CREAMY FRUIT PIE FILLING

Equipment:
mixing bowl
electric mixer (optional)
mixing spoon
measuring cup
measuring spoons

Ingredients:
1 cup plain yogurt or sour cream
1 8-ounce package cream cheese
$\frac{1}{4}$ cup honey
$\frac{1}{4}$ tsp. vanilla or orange extract
$1\frac{1}{2}$ cups chopped fresh fruit—
peaches, berries, pineapple, grapes, nectarines, pears

Method:
1. Combine cream cheese and 3 Tbsps. of the yogurt or sour cream in mixing bowl and beat until smooth.
2. Beat in the remaining yogurt or sour cream, honey, and extract.
3. Pour filling into graham-cracker pie crust and freeze for several hours.
4. When pie is ready to be served, decorate the top with the chopped fruit or berries.

In some countries, a loud burp is considered a polite way of expressing appreciation for a good meal. In this country a nice thank you seems to be more appreciated.

CHOCOLATE MOUSSE
PIE FILLING ALSO
MAKES A DELICIOUS
PUDDING DISHED
INTO INDIVIDUAL
SERVING
BOWLS

FLUFFY FRUIT PIE FILLING

Equipment:

small saucepan with lid
electric blender
large mixing bowl
electric mixer or eggbeater
measuring cup
rubber spatula

Ingredients:

$1\frac{1}{4}$ cups dried fruit—prunes, apricots, peaches, pears, or pineapple—alone or mixed
$1\frac{1}{4}$ cups water
$\frac{1}{3}$ cup honey
juice of $\frac{1}{2}$ lemon
1 tsp. cinnamon
2 cups heavy cream
1 prepared graham-cracker pie crust

Method:

1. Combine dried fruit and water in saucepan, cover, and place over high heat. As soon as the water comes to a boil, reduce heat to medium and simmer for 12 minutes.

2. Remove pan from heat and scrape fruit into blender. Add honey, lemon juice, and cinnamon and whiz on high speed (press the "puree" button if your blender has it) until the fruit is smooth and saucy.

3. In the mixing bowl, whip the heavy cream. Gently stir in the fruit mixture until the two elements are *thoroughly* blended.

4. Pour the fruit filling into the pie crust and chill in the freezer for about 1 hour, or until firm, before serving.

CHOCOLATE MOUSSE PIE FILLING

Equipment:

double boiler
2 large mixing bowls   measuring spoons
electric mixer   rubber spatula

Ingredients:

5 eggs
5 ounces (5 squares) semi-sweet baking chocolate
2 Tbsps. water, apricot nectar, or orange juice
1 Tbsp. honey
1 tsp. vanilla
dash of salt
1 prepared graham-cracker pie crust

Marvelous Mousse Add-Ins:

1 banana, finely sliced
$\frac{1}{4}$ cup shredded coconut
$\frac{1}{4}$ cup raisins and $\frac{1}{4}$ cup chopped nuts
1 small can mandarin oranges, substituting its juice for liquid listed above

Method:

1. Separate egg whites and egg yolks into the two large mixing bowls.

2. Melt chocolate squares in top half of double boiler.

3. Scrape melted chocolate into the bowl containing the egg yolks and add liquid, honey, vanilla, and salt. Beat ingredients on low speed of electric mixer until the batter is all brown and smooth.

4. Clean mixer blades under warm water and then beat the egg whites until stiff. Fold them into the chocolate mixture. Continue to fold until the two elements are *thoroughly* blended.

5. If you choose, gently stir in one of the Marvelous Add-Ins.

6. Pour Mousse into the pie crust or into individual serving bowls. Place in the refrigerator and chill for at least one hour before serving. For a real thrill, top off with freshly whipped cream.

PEANUT BUTTER or SESAME PAN COOKIES

Equipment:
large skillet or electric frying pan
mixing bowl
mixing spoon
measuring cup
measuring spoons
metal spatula

Ingredients:
$\frac{1}{2}$ cup butter, softened
$\frac{1}{2}$ cup brown sugar
$\frac{1}{2}$ cup peanut butter or tahini
2 eggs
1 tsp. vanilla extract
1 cup whole-wheat flour
$\frac{1}{2}$ cup raisins

Method:

1. In mixing bowl, cream together butter and brown sugar.
2. Stir in the peanut butter or tahini and mix until smooth.
3. Add eggs and vanilla and beat until smooth.
4. Stir flour and salt into batter. When well mixed, add the raisins and stir again.
5. Place skillet over medium heat, or turn the electric frying pan temperature dial to 350°. Drop cookie batter by rounded teaspoons onto hot surface and cook both sides until brown, about 3-4 minutes on each side.

TO KEEP YOUR COOKIEs CRISP, STORE THEM IN A TIGHT-LIDDED JAR OR OTHER CONTAINER.

If you can't brush your teeth after a meal, eat an apple, then suck on a lemon or chew a sprig of parsley. The apple helps remove food particles while lemon & parsley sweeten the breath.

CHOCOLATE CHIP COOKIES

Equipment:

large skillet or electric frying pan
mixing bowl
mixing spoon
measuring cup
measuring spoons
metal spatula

Ingredients:

$\frac{1}{2}$ cup brown sugar
$\frac{1}{2}$ cup butter, softened
2 eggs
2 Tbsps. water
1 tsp. vanilla extract
1 cup whole-wheat flour or
    unbleached white flour
$\frac{1}{2}$ tsp. salt
1 6-ounce package choco-
    late chips
$\frac{1}{2}$ cup chopped nuts (optional)

Method:

1. In mixing bowl, cream together sugar and butter.
2. Add the eggs, water, and vanilla, and beat until smooth.
3. Stir the flour and salt into batter. When well mixed, add the
   chocolate chips and nuts and
   stir again.
4. Place skillet over medium
   heat, or turn the electric frying
   pan temperature dial to 350°.
   Drop cookie batter by
   rounded teaspoons onto hot
   surface and cook both sides
   until brown, about 3–4 minutes on each side.

OATMEAL COOKIES

Equipment:

large skillet or electric frying pan
2 mixing bowls
mixing spoon
measuring cup
measuring spoons
metal spatula

Ingredients:

2 cups uncooked oats
$\frac{3}{4}$ cup whole-wheat flour or
    unbleached white flour
1 tsp. cinnamon
$\frac{1}{2}$ tsp. salt
$\frac{1}{2}$ cup butter, softened
1 cup brown sugar
2 eggs
2 Tbsps. water
1 tsp. vanilla extract
$\frac{1}{2}$ cup raisins

Tasty Oatmeal Cookie Additions:

$\frac{1}{2}$ cup chopped nuts
$\frac{1}{2}$ cup shredded coconut
$\frac{1}{2}$ cup sunflower seeds

Method:

1. Combine oats, flour, cinnamon, and salt in mixing bowl.
2. In the other mixing bowl,
   cream together butter and
   sugar. Add eggs, water, and
   vanilla. Stir until well
   blended.
3. Stir oat mixture into sugar
   mixture and mix well. Add
   raisins and any Tasty Oatmeal
   Cookie Additions.
4. Place skillet over medium
   heat or turn the electric frying
   pan temperature dial to 350°.
   Drop cookie batter by
   rounded teaspoons onto hot
   surface and cook both sides
   until brown, about 4 minutes
   on each side.

these recipes make about 30

MAKE YOUR OWN ICE CREAM SANDWICHES BY PUTTING YOUR FAVORITE ICE CREAM BETWEEN 2 BIG COOKIES.

FORTUNE COOKIES

Equipment:

mixing bowl
mixing spoon
measuring spoons
small skillet or electric frying pan
metal spatula
cookie sheet

Ingredients:

4 Tbsps. unbleached white flour
2 Tbsps. brown sugar
1 Tbsp. cornstarch
dash of salt
2 Tbsps. vegetable oil
1 egg white
3 Tbsps. water
$\frac{1}{2}$ tsp. grated orange or lemon peel; or $\frac{1}{4}$ tsp. ground fennel, cardamom, or anise seed

Method:

1. In mixing bowl, stir together the flour, brown sugar, cornstarch, and salt.
2. Add vegetable oil and egg white and stir until smooth.
3. Add water and grated citrus peel or spice and stir again.
4. Grease the skillet or frying pan and place over medium heat or set on 325°.
5. As soon as the skillet is heated, drop a tablespoon of batter onto it and rotate skillet so that batter spreads into a thin, 3½-inch circle. Cook for 4 minutes, turn batter over, and cook 2 minutes more.
6. Working quickly, remove batter and place the fortune across the center of the cookie, fold in half, then bend slightly over the edge of the mixing bowl (or another clean bowl). Set cookies on cookie sheet to cool.

First, write fortunes on separate slips of paper.

Place a fortune across each cookie.

fold cookie in half.

fold it slightly again.

these things are so silly!

Your face will one day be seen by thousands in the pages of a cookbook.

83

ICE CREAM CONES

Equipment:
mixing bowl
mixing spoon
measuring cup
measuring spoons
small skillet or electric frying pan
metal spatula
cookie sheet   wooden toothpicks

Ingredients:
$\frac{1}{4}$ cup unbleached white flour
2 Tbsps. brown sugar
1 Tbsp. cornstarch
dash of salt
2 Tbsps. vegetable oil
1 egg white
3 Tbsps. water
$\frac{1}{4}$ tsp. vanilla extract or $\frac{1}{8}$ tsp. almond, lemon, or orange extract

Ice-Cream Cone Add-Ins:
1 tsp. shredded coconut
1 tsp. finely ground nuts
$\frac{1}{8}$ tsp. fennel seeds
1 tsp. wheat germ

Method:
1. In mixing bowl, blend together the flour, brown sugar, cornstarch, and salt.
2. Add the vegetable oil and egg white and stir until smooth.
3. Add water, flavor extract, and any Add-Ins you want. Stir again.
4. Grease skillet or electric frying pan. Put over low heat or set on 300°. When it is hot, pour on 2 Tbsps. of batter and rotate skillet so that batter spreads in a thin, 5-inch circle. Fry cones one at a time.
5. Cook batter for 5 minutes on one side, lift with spatula, and cook 2 minutes on other.
6. Working quickly, roll the batter into a cone shape and secure the overlapping edge with several toothpicks. Cool on the cookie sheet. Remove toothpicks when cones are crispy and cool.
7. For each successive cone, spread a little more vegetable oil on the skillet.

SAUCES
CHOCOLATE
FUDGE
BUTTERSCOTH
FRUIT FLAVORS

NUTS
PEANUTS
WALNUTS
ALMONDS
PECANS
CASHEWS
HAZELNUTS
FILBERTS
CHESTNUTS
BRAZIL NUTS

INVENT YOUR OWN SUNDAE

Make a deliciously dazzling dessert with your favorite ice cream and one of these Super Sundae Toppings. Set out an array of different toppings, give everyone a bowl of ice cream, and let them help themselves. There's no end to the different kinds of sundaes you can make.

NATURAL SYRUPS

MAPLE SYRUP
HONEY
MOLASSES
SORGHUM

DRIED FRUITS

RAISINS
CURRANTS
DATES
FIGS
APRICOTS
PRUNES

FRESH FRUITS

BERRIES
BANANAS
PEACHES
PINEAPPLE
GRAPES
MELON BALLS
CHERRIES

VARIOUS OTHER GOOD THINGS

PEANUT BUTTER
JELLY OR JAM
CHOCOLATE CHIPS
GRANOLA
SHREDDED COCONUT
TOASTED WHEAT GERM
COCOA   CAROB POWD

CINNAMON
POWDERED MALT
WHIPPED CREAM

HOMEMADE CARAMEL

Put an unopened can of sweetened condensed milk in a medium-size sauce pan. Cover with water and bring to a boil. Reduce heat and simmer for 2½ hours. Then turn off the heat, leaving the can in the pan. When the water cools remove the can and open. Delicious

STOPPING SODA POP TOP POPPING

MAKING YOUR OWN DRINKS

There are as many different special drinks as there are ways of getting thirsty, and with these recipes, you can make lots of them. They require only a little more effort than it takes to flip a soda-pop lid, and the extra good taste is worth it. These recipes make enough for one extremely parched person, two quite thirsty people, or three slightly dry individuals.

To get the most juice out of a lemon, before cutting it press it hard against the counter with the palm of your hand and roll it back & forth.

86

COLD BLENDER DRINKS
5¢

Place all the ingredients in the blender jar. Cover and whiz on medium speed until well blended. If you want ice in your drink, remove the center of the cover and, while the blender is on, drop in 3 or 4 pieces, and blend until they're completely crushed. Pour into one tall, two medium, or three short glasses and drink up.

BERRY-BERRY

1 cup berries
1 cup milk
1 Tbsp. honey

BLACK & BLUE BERRIES

1 cup blackberries or blueberries
1 cup soda water
2 Tbsps. honey or sugar
1 tsp. lemon juice

EARTH SHAKE

A drink to chew
1½ cups pineapple juice
½ cup crushed pineapple
1 large carrot, peeled and chopped

COOL COW

To make this really cool, add a handful of ice.
2 cups milk
½ tsp. almond extract
4 tsps. honey or maple syrup

PEANUT BUTTER SHAKE

2 cups milk, or 1 cup milk and 2 scoops ice cream (any flavor)
⅓ cup peanut butter
1 Tbsp. molasses or honey
dash of cinnamon

87

MORE COLD BLENDER DRINKS

FRUIT FLIP-FLOP

1 cup yogurt
1 cup fruit juice
(cranapple is
incredible)

PINEAPPLE POWER

1 small can pineapple
slices with juice
2 cups water
1 Tbsp. honey
$\frac{1}{4}$ tsp. ginger

JUNGLE JUICE

1 banana, broken
into chunks
2 cups orange juice
dash of ginger

NUTS ABOUT MILK

*Blend this one a
little longer—about
the time it takes to
sing three rounds of
"Row, Row, Row
Your Boat."*
2 cups milk
small handful of
almonds or
cashews
2 Tbsps. shredded
coconut
1 Tbsp. honey

PINEAPPLE UPSIDE-DOWN SHAKE

1 cup yogurt or 2
scoops ice cream
(any flavor)
$\frac{1}{2}$ cup milk
1 small can
pineapple chunks
and juice
1 tsp. honey (only
if you use yogurt)
$\frac{1}{4}$ tsp. cinnamon

YOGURT COOLER

*Be sure to use lots of
ice in this drink. It's
great on a hot day.*
1 cup yogurt
1 cup fresh, frozen,
or canned fruit—
peaches,
blueberries,
strawberries, or
other

88

APPLE KARATE

Another chewy drink
2 cups apple juice
   or cider
1 large carrot,
   peeled and
   chopped

DUTCH TREAT

2 cups milk
2 Tbsps. carob
   powder or cocoa
$\frac{1}{2}$ tsp. vanilla
   extract
2 Tbsps. honey
$\frac{1}{2}$ tsp. cinnamon

MUSH MELON

2 cups melon pieces
   (any kind but
   watermelon)
2 cups water
1 Tbsp. honey
1 tsp. lemon juice

STRAWBERRY SHIVERS

$1\frac{1}{2}$ cups fresh strawberries plus
4 tsps. honey, or
1 10-ounce pack-
   age frozen
   strawberries
$1\frac{1}{2}$ cups water

RAINBOW

1 cup yogurt or 2
   scoops ice cream
   (any flavor)
1 cup fruit juice,
   any kind
1 cup chopped fresh
   fruit, any kind

MONKEY BUSINESS

1 cup yogurt or 2
   scoops ice cream
   (any flavor)
1 cup milk
1 banana, broken
   into chunks
2 Tbsps. carob
   powder or cocoa
2 Tbsps. honey
   (only if you use
   yogurt)
dash of nutmeg or
   cinnamon

SWEET BANANAS

2 cups milk
1 banana, broken
   into chunks
1 Tbsp. honey or
   molasses

VERY NICE ICE

Freeze any favorite juice in an ice-cube tray. Use these in drinks instead of regular ice cubes, or chop them in an electric blender to make a delicious slush.

OTHER COLD DRINKS

No blender is needed for these drinks . . .
just a small pitcher . . .
a big spoon to stir with . . .
and if you want, lots of ice!

CRAZY COW

1 cup apple juice
1 cup milk

MELLOW YELLOW

1 cup apricot nectar
1 cup pineapple juice
dash of ginger

JUST A MOOMINT

2 cups milk
chocolate syrup—you decide how much
$\frac{1}{4}$ tsp. mint flavoring

GRAPPLE

1 cup grape juice
1 cup cider or apple juice
1 tsp. lemon juice
1/4 tsp. cinnamon

GREAT GRAPES

1 cup grape juice
1 cup soda water
1 Tbsp. honey or sugar
1 Tbsp. lemon juice

ORANGATANG

1 cup orange juice
1 cup cranberry juice

LEMONADE

The canned kind can't
compare to this!
2 cups plain or soda water
1/2 cup lemon juice
2 or more Tbsps. honey

TOMATO TANG

2 cups tomato or V-8 juice
big squeeze of lemon juice
dash of celery salt

PLANTATION PUNCH

1 1/2 cups orange juice
1/2 cup lemon juice
2 Tbsps. molasses
dash of powdered cloves
sprig of fresh mint (if
you happen to have
one handy)

GRAPES IN A BOG

1 cup grape juice
1 cup cranberry juice
dash each of cinnamon
and cloves

NUT NOG

2 cups milk
⅓ cup nut butter—peanut
butter, cashew butter,
or almond butter
1 Tbsp. honey
sprinkle of nutmeg

HOT DRINKS

HOT LEMONADE

If you drink this one while bundled up in bed, it's supposed to help cure a cold.
2 cups water
½ cup lemon juice
2 or more Tbsps. honey
½ tsp. ginger

Hint for heating milk:
First rinse the pan in
cold water. This keeps
the milk from sticking
to the pan.

Put all the ingredients
in a saucepan and stir
until well blended.
Warm over low to
medium heat, stirring
occasionally, until liquid
is hot but not boiling.
Pour into a mug.

MAPLE TODDY

2 cups milk
1 Tbsp. maple syrup
dash of nutmeg

MOLASSES TODDY

2 cups milk
1 Tbsp. molasses
½ tsp. rum flavoring

MIKE TODDY

2 cups milk
4 tsps. honey
½ tsp. almond extract
dash of spice—nutmeg,
cinnamon, or allspice

CIDER DELIGHTER

2 cups cider or
apple juice
2 whole cloves or dash
of powdered cloves
1 cinnamon stick or
½ tsp. powdered
cinnamon

HOT CHOCOLATE

2 cups milk
2 Tbsps. carob powder
or cocoa
2 Tbsps. honey or
maple syrup
½ tsp. vanilla extract
½ tsp. cinnamon
marshmallows (if you
must)

Warm milk
is a good
drink to have
before going
to bed. It is
a natural
tranquilizer.

93

INDEX OF RECIPES

Jane Cooper and Sherry Streeter first discovered their mutual love of kitchens as roommates in New Haven, Connecticut, six years ago. Since then, their lives have gone in diverse directions—but their love for food lingers on!

Jane Cooper now lives in Randolph Center, Vermont, a town of six hundred, where she is involved in photography and journalism, garden mulching, wine making, and enjoying country living. She is presently at work on a forthcoming book on woodstove cooking.

Sherry Streeter has worked in the art world as designer, teacher, and artist, and has been a full-time free-lance illustrator since 1972. She lives in New Haven, Connecticut and, when not drawing, spends time sailing, hiking, skiing, and munching Gorp.